Defoe Abbott Marx Hardy Montaigne Machiavelli Haggard Chesterton Cooper Emerson Joyce Austen Hugo Eliot Grimm
Melville Stoker Carroll Christie Maupassant Byron Schiller Smith Kafka Hall
Wilde Garnett Einstein Fitzgerald Engels Hawthorne Willis
Goethe Dostoyevsky
Cotton Kipling Doyle
Baum Henry Nietzsche Balzac
Leslie Dumas Flaubert Turgenev Crane
Stockton Vatsyayana Verne
Burroughs Vinci
Curtis Tocqueville Gogol Busch
Homer Widger Tolstoy Whitman
Darwin Thoreau Twain Scott Harte
Potter Freud Zola Lawrence Dickens Plato Hesse
Kant Jowett Stevenson Burton
Andersen Cervantes
London Descartes Voltaire Cooke
Poe Aristotle Wells Irving
Hale James Hastings
Bunner Shakespeare
Richter Chambers da Chekhov Shaw Wodehouse Benedict Alcott
Doré Dante Swift Pushkin Newton

Raphael A Collection Of Fifteen Pictures And A Portrait Of The Painter With Introduction And Interpretation

Estelle M. (Estelle May) Hurll

Imprint

This book is part of TREDITION CLASSICS

Author: Estelle M. (Estelle May) Hurll
Cover design: Buchgut, Berlin – Germany

Publisher: tredition GmbH, Hamburg - Germany
ISBN: 978-3-8472-2895-0

www.tredition.com
www.tredition.de

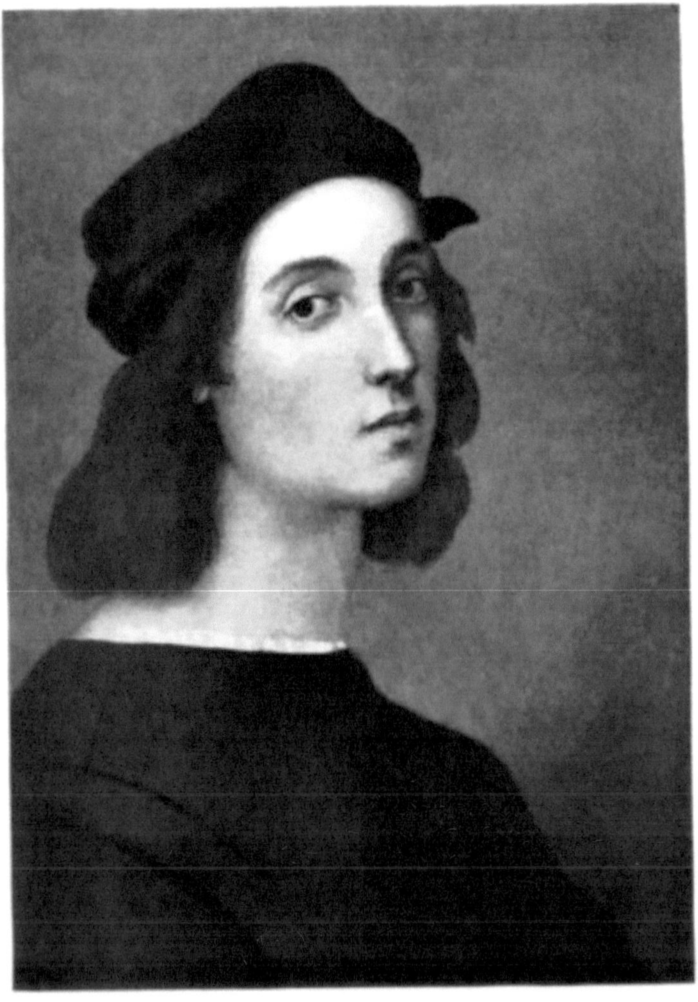

RAPHAEL SANZIO D' URBINO (BY HIMSELF)
Uffizi Gallery, Florence

RAPHAEL

A COLLECTION OF FIFTEEN PICTURES

AND A PORTRAIT OF THE PAINTER

WITH INTRODUCTION AND

INTERPRETATION

EDITED BY

ESTELLE M. HURLL

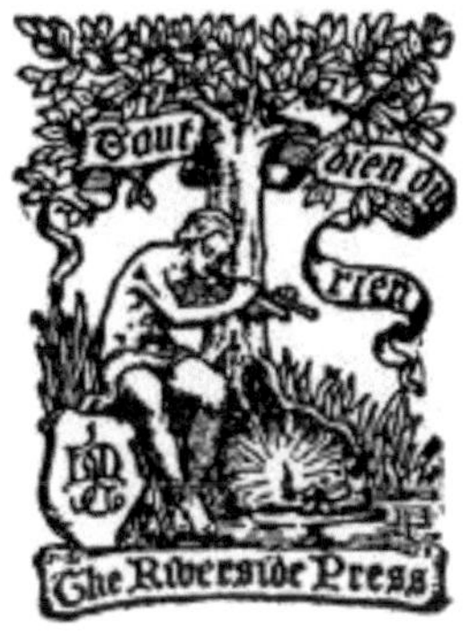

PREFACE

The object of this collection of prints is to introduce the student to Raphael through the pictures which appeal directly to the imagination with some story interest. With this characteristic as the leading principle of choice, the variety of subjects is perhaps as wide as the conditions admit. No attempt is made to represent all the sides of the painter's art; his portraits are ignored and his Madonnas inadequately represented, in order to give place to pictures which awaken as many points of interest as possible. Within these narrow limits Raphael, as an illustrator and a composer, is even in these few pictures clearly represented.

Had choice been limited to pictures painted throughout by Raphael himself, the value of the collection would have been seriously affected, as some of the master's most interesting works were handed over to his pupils for execution. Our list, however, contains only such works as are at this date reckoned indisputably to be from Raphael's own designs.

The text has only the modest aim of making the pictures intelligible. Critical explanations are beyond its scope, and historical data are for the most part relegated to the accompanying tables. The Introduction is intended for teachers, and contains suggestions for a comparative study of the pictures which may be carried out at discretion.

All the reproductions in this book are from photographs made directly from the original paintings. In order to get the best results a careful comparison was made of the work of leading photographers. The photographer of each picture is mentioned in the Table of Contents.

ESTELLE M. HURLL.

New Bedford, Mass.

June, 1899.

CONTENTS AND LIST OF PICTURES

[vii]

INTRODUCTION

I. ON RAPHAEL'S CHARACTER AS AN ARTIST.

No one of the old Italian masters has taken such a firm hold upon the popular imagination as Raphael. Other artists wax and wane in public favor as they are praised by one generation of critics or disparaged by the next; but Raphael's name continues to stand in public estimation as that of the favorite painter in Christendom. The passing centuries do not dim his fame, though he is subjected to severe criticism; and he continues, as he began, the first love of the people.

The subjects of his pictures are nearly all of a cheerful nature. He exercised his skill for the most part on scenes which were agreeable to contemplate. Pain and ugliness were strangers to his art; he was preëminently the artist of joy. This is to be referred not only to his pleasure-loving nature, but to the great influence upon him of the rediscovery of Greek art in his day, an art which dealt distinctively with objects of delight.

Moreover Raphael is compassionate towards mind as well as heart; he requires of us neither too strenuous feeling nor too much thinking. As his subjects do not overtax the sympathies with harrowing emotions, neither does his art overtax the understanding with complicated effects. His pictures are apparently so simple that they demand no great intellectual effort and no technical education to [viii] enjoy them. He does all the work for us, and his art is too perfect to astonish. It was not his way to show what difficult things he could do, but he made it appear that great art is the easiest thing in the world. This ease was, however, the result of a splendid mastery of his art. Thus he arranges the fifty-two figures in the School of Athens, or the three figures of the Madonna of the Chair, so simply and unobtrusively that we might imagine such feats were an everyday affair. Yet in both cases he solves most difficult problems of composition with a success scarcely paralleled in the history of art.

Even the Master himself seldom achieved the same kind of success twice. His Parnassus lacks the variety of the School of Athens, though the single figures have a similar grace, and the Incendio del

Borgo or Conflagration in the Borgo, with groups equal in beauty to any in the other two frescoes, has not the unity of either. Again, while the Parnassus and the Liberation of Peter show a masterly adaptation to extremely awkward spaces, the Transfiguration fails to solve a much easier problem of composition.

Preferring by an instinct such as the Greek artist possessed, the statuesque effects of repose to the portrayal of action, Raphael showed himself capable of both. The Hellenic calm of Parnassus is not more impressive than the splendid charge of the avenging spirits upon Heliodorus; the visionary idealism of the angel-led Peter is matched by the vigorous realism of Peter called from his fishing to the apostleship; the brooding quiet of maternity expressed in the Madonna of the Chair has a perfect complement in the alert activity of the swiftly moving Sistine Madonna.

Great as was Raphael's achievement in many directions, he is remembered above all else as a painter of Madonnas. [ix] Here was the subject best expressing the individuality of his genius. From the beginning to the end of his career the sweet mystery of motherhood never ceased to fascinate him. Again and again he sounded the depths of maternal experience, always making some new discovery.

The Madonna of the Chair emphasizes most prominently, perhaps, the physical instincts of maternity. "She bends over the child," says Taine, "with the beautiful action of a wild animal." Like a mother creature instinctively protecting her young, she gathers him in her capacious embrace as if to shield him from some impending danger. The Sistine Madonna, on the other hand, is the most spiritual of Raphael's creations, the perfect embodiment of ideal womanhood. The mother's love is here transfigured by the spirit of sacrifice. Forgetful of self, and obedient to the heavenly summons, she bears her son forth to the service of humanity.

Sister spirits of the Madonnas, and hardly second in delicate loveliness, are the virgin saints of Raphael; the Catherine, the Cecilia, the Magdalene, and the Barbara are abiding ideals in our dreams of fair women.

The same sweetness of nature which prompted Raphael's fondness for lovely women and happy children shows itself also in his delineation of angels. The archangel Michael, the angel visitors of

Abraham, and the celestial spirits appearing to Heliodorus all follow closely upon the Madonnas in the purity and serenity of their beauty. In the same fellowship also belongs the beautiful youth in the crowd at Lystra, who is as sharply contrasted with his surroundings as if he were a denizen of another sphere. The ideal is again repeated in the St. John of the Cecilia altar-piece, whose uplifted face has a sweetness which is not so much feminine as celestial. The angel of Peter's deliverance is less successful than the artist's other angel [x] types. The head seems too small for the splendidly vigorous body, and the face lacks somewhat of strength.

If Raphael's favorite ideals were drawn from youth and womanhood, it was not because he did not understand the purely masculine. The Æneas of the Borgo fresco, the Paul of the Cecilia altar-piece, and the Sixtus of the Sistine Madonna show, in three ages, what is best and most distinctive in ideal manhood.

Raphael's type of beauty is not such as calls forth immediate or extravagant admiration: it is satisfying rather than amazing, and its qualities dawn slowly though steadily upon the imagination. Raphael holds always to the golden mean; no exaggerated note jars upon the perfection of his harmonies. For this reason his pictures never grow tiresome. They stand the test of daily companionship and grow ever lovelier through familiarity.

Without forcing the parallel, we may say that something of the same spirit which animated the work of Raphael reappears in the familiar poetry of Longfellow. The one artist had an eye for beautiful line, the other had an ear for melodious verse, and both alike shunned whatever was inharmonious, always seeking grace and symmetry. Their subjects were, indeed, of dissimilar range. Raphael, impressed by the scholarship of his time, chose themes which were larger and more related to the experience of the world, while Longfellow was never very far removed from the golden milestone of domestic life. Yet in diverse subjects both turned instinctively to aspects of womanhood, to what was refined and gently emotional, and turned away from the violent and revolutionary.

[xi]

II. ON BOOKS OF REFERENCE.

Within the last forty years the methods of criticism as applied to art have undergone so many changes that there has been a rapid succession of biographers and critics of Raphael until the student reader of to-day scarcely knows whom to believe. The time was when Vasari, in his important "Lives of the Painters," was the accepted source of information, and all current writers borrowed unquestioningly from him both facts and opinions; but the old chronicler was too often influenced by popular gossip and personal prejudice to be depended upon. Many of his stories are positively disproved by documentary evidence, and for some years he has stood in dust and disgrace on the upper shelves of the bookcase. From this exile a revised edition has recently brought him forth to fresh honors. The joint work of Mr. and Mrs. E. H. Blashfield with A. A. Hopkins has given us an annotated text which we may read with equal pleasure and profit. This is certainly the best of all reference books to put us in touch with the period in which Raphael lived.

The German work on Raphael by Passavant, once so weighty, is now useful only to those who have opportunity to compare it with other authorities. So likewise the work of Crowe and Cavalcaselle is no longer desirable as a sole authority. Even the splendid work of Eugene Müntz (translated by Walter Armstrong), the latest and most valuable of the comprehensive books on Raphael, must be read in the light of later criticism. Müntz's volume contains a complete list of the master's works, — frescoes, easel pictures, tapestries, drawings, and works in architecture and sculpture, — each class subdivided according to subject.

A few of the shorter biographies of Raphael have been corrected according to the conclusions of the most recent [xii] critical scholarship, as represented by Morelli. Notable among these is the life of Raphael in Kugler's "Handbook of the Italian Schools," revised by A. H. Layard, and the life of Raphael included in Mrs. Jameson's "Early Italian Painters," revised by Estelle M. Hurll.

The latest entirely new short biographies of Raphael are those (1) by Mrs. Henry Ady (Julia Cartwright), issued in two parts as monographs for "The Portfolio:" the "Early Work of Raphael" and "Raphael in Rome," and (2) by H. Knackfuss in a series of German "Künstler-Monographien" (also published in an English translation). Both are well illustrated and useful books.

Finally the student is referred to Bernhard Berenson's "Central Italian Painters of the Renaissance" for an exceedingly valuable estimate of Raphael's character as an artist.

Many books have been written on the separate works of Raphael,—the Vatican frescoes, the cartoons, the Madonnas, etc.,—but as most of these are in German and Italian they are not generally available. The Blashfield Vasari enumerates a long list of them in the Bibliography preceding the "Life of Raphael."

III. HISTORICAL DIRECTORY OF THE PICTURES OF THIS COLLECTION.

Portrait frontispiece. Painted on wood, 1506, as a gift from the painter to his uncle, Simone Ciarla, of Urbino. In 1588 the portrait passed from Urbino to the Academy of St. Luke, Rome. Later it was sold to Cardinal Leopoldo de' Medici for the Hall of Portraits of the Old Masters in the Uffizi Gallery, Florence.

1. *The Madonna of the Chair* is a wood panel 2 ft. 4-3/4 in. diameter. It was painted between 1510-1514, and is now in the Pitti Gallery, Florence.

2. *Abraham and the Three Angels* is a mural painting in [xiii] the fourth arcade of the Loggie, Vatican Palace, Rome. It was executed by Francesco Penni.

3, 4. *The Miraculous Draught of Fishes* and *The Sacrifice at Lystra* are cartoons in distemper colors. The execution was by Raphael's pupils in 1515-1516. They were sent to Flanders as designs for tapestries, and discovered by Rubens in a manufactory at Arras, 1630; Charles I. of England purchased them, and they are now in the South Kensington Museum, London.

5. *Heliodorus driven from the Temple* (detail of the larger composition known by this name) is a mural painting which gives the name to the Camera d' Eliodoro, Vatican Palace, Rome. The date of the painting is 1511-1512.

6. *The Liberation of Peter* is a mural painting in the Camera d' Eliodoro, Vatican Palace, Rome; the execution is by Giulio Romano, 1514.

7. *The Holy Family of Francis I.* is a canvas panel 8 ft. 9 in. by 5 ft. 3 in., painted for Lorenzo de' Medici, and presented by the Pope Leo X. to Francis I. of France; hence the name. It was executed by Giulio Romano in 1518, and is now in the Louvre, Paris.

8. *St. Catherine of Alexandria* is a wood panel 2 ft. 4 in. by I ft. 9-1/2 in., painted in 1507, and now in the National Gallery, London.

9. *St. Cecilia* is a panel painting which was transferred from wood to canvas. It was painted about 1516 for the Church of S. Giovanni a Monte, Bologna, and is now in the Bologna Gallery.

10. *The Transfiguration*, 14 ft. 9 in. by 9 ft. 1-1/2 in. Raphael painted the upper part in 1519, and the picture was finished after his death by Giulio Romano. It was ordered by the Cardinal de' Medici for the Cathedral at Narbonne (France), but was retained in Rome after the artist's death. It was taken to Paris during the French Revolution, and restored to Rome in 1815. It is now in the Vatican Gallery.

11. *Parnassus* is a mural painting in the Camera della Segnatura, Vatican Palace, Rome. The date is 1509-1511.

12. *Socrates and Alcibiades* (detail of the School of Athens) [xiv] is a mural painting in the Camera della Segnatura, Vatican Palace, Rome. It was painted in 1509-1511.

13. *The Flight of Æneas* (detail of the Conflagration in the Borgo), a mural painting in the Camera dell' Incendio, Vatican Palace, Rome. It was executed by Giulio Romano about 1515.

14. *St. Michael slaying the Dragon*, a panel 8 ft. 9-1/2 in. by 5 ft. 3 in. It was painted on wood and transferred to canvas. It was ordered by Leo X. as a gift to Francis I., and was presented to him by Lorenzo de' Medici. The execution is by Giulio Romano, 1518. It is now in the Louvre, Paris.

15. *The Sistine Madonna*, a canvas panel 8 ft. 8 in. by 6 ft. 5 in., was painted about 1515 for the high altar of the Church of St. Sixtus, Piacenza, and received its name from the portrait figure of St. Sixtus

which it contains; it was purchased by the Elector of Saxony in 1753-1754 for the Dresden Gallery.

IV. COLLATERAL READINGS FROM LITERATURE.

In connection with St. Catherine: —

Latin Hymn, Vox Sonora Nostri Chori, St. Catherine's Day. Translated by David Morgan.

Mrs. Jameson. Sacred and Legendary Art.

S. Baring-Gould. Lives of the Saints. Volume for November.

In connection with St. Cecilia: —

S. Baring-Gould. Lives of the Saints. Volume for November.

Mrs. Jameson. Sacred and Legendary Art.

Chaucer. Second Nonnes Tale.

Dryden. Alexander's Feast: Ode in honor of St. Cecilia's Day.

In connection with Parnassus: —

Shelley. Hymn of Apollo.

Keats. Ode to Apollo.

Bulfinch. Age of Fable.

In connection with the Flight of Æneas: —

Virgil. Æneid, Book II. Translated by C. P. Cranch.

In connection with Socrates and Alcibiades: —

[xv]

Fénelon. Lives of the Philosophers. Translated by John Cormack.

Plato. Alcibiades, The Symposium, Protagoras. Translated by Jowett.

Milton. Paradise Regained. Book IV. lines 240-285.

In connection with St. Michael and the Dragon: —

Milton. Paradise Lost. Book VI.

In connection with the Sistine Madonna: —

Mrs. Jameson. Sacred and Legendary Art (for St. Barbara).

V. OUTLINE TABLE OF THE PRINCIPAL EVENTS IN RAPHAEL'S LIFE.

1483. Raphael born at Urbino.

1499. Raphael enters Perugino's studio at Perugia.

1504. "The Marriage of the Virgin."

1504. Raphael's first visit to Florence.

1505. Raphael in Perugia:—

The Madonna of St. Anthony.

The fresco of San Severo.

1506. Visit at Urbino:—

Raphael's portrait by himself.

1504-1508. The Florentine Period:—

Granduca Madonna.

Tempi Madonna.

Madonna in the Meadow.

The Madonna del Cardellino.

The Belle Jardiniere.

The Canigiani Madonna.

1508. Raphael called to Rome by Pope Julius II.

1511. Raphael frescoes the Camera della Segnatura.

1512. Raphael begins decoration of the Camera d' Eliodoro.

1513. Raphael commissioned by Leo X. to continue work begun under Julius II.

1514. "Galatea."

1514. Raphael appointed architect of St. Peter's by Leo X.

1508-1515. Some Madonnas of the Roman Period:—

Foligno Madonna.

[xvi]

Garvagh Madonna.

The Madonna of Casa Alba.

The Madonna of the Chair.

The Sistine Madonna.

1515. Camera dell' Incendio completed under Raphael's direction.

1515-1516. Cartoons for tapestries executed under Raphael's direction.

1517. Farnesina frescoes painted under Raphael's direction.

1519. The Transfiguration.

1520. Raphael died in Rome.

VI. SOME FAMOUS CONTEMPORARIES OF RAPHAEL.

IN ITALY.

Rulers:—

Lorenzo de' Medici (reigned 1469-1492) and Pietro de' Medici (1492-1494), dukes of Florence.

Giovanni Galeazzo Sforza (reigned 1476-1494), Lodovico Maria Sforza (1494-1500), and Massimiliano Sforza (1512-1515), dukes of Milan.

Francesco Maria della Rovere, duke of Urbino (born 1490; died 1535).

Ferdinand I. (reigned 1458-1494), Ferdinand II. (reigned 1495-1496), and Ferdinand III., kings of Naples, the last being he who was also king of Spain as Ferdinand V.

Innocent VIII. (1484-1492), Alexander VI. (1492-1503), Pius III. (1503), Julius II. (1503-1513), and Leo X. (1513-1523), popes.

Painters:—

Older group:—

Perugino (1446-1523).

Bazzi (1477-1549).

Leonardo da Vinci (1452-1519).

Bartolommeo (1475-1517).

Giorgione (1477-1510).

Titian (1477-1576).

Giovanni Bellini (1428-1516).

Compeers:—

Andrea del Sarto (1486-1531). [xvii]

Sebastian del Piombo (1485-1547).

Assistants and Pupils:—

Giulio Romano (1492-1546).

Giovanni da Udine (1487-1564).

Francesco Penni (1488-1528).

Marc Antonio (1487-1539), engraver.

Michelangelo (1474-1564), sculptor.

Bramante (1444-1514), architect of St. Peter's.

Sanazzaro Jacopo (1458-1530 or 1532), poet (De Partu Virginia).

Ariosto (1474-1533), poet (Orlando Furioso).

Francesco Berni (1496-1536), comic poet.

Cardinal Bembi (1470-1547), celebrated scholar.

Count Baldasarre Castiglione (1478-1529), writer and patron of literature.

Christopher Columbus (1436 or 1446-1506), discoverer.

IN PORTUGAL.

Vasco da Gama (died 1525), discoverer.

IN ENGLAND.

Richard III. (1483-1485), Henry VII. (1485-1509), Henry VIII. (1509-1547), kings.

Sebastian Cabot (1477-15?), discoverer.

IN GERMANY.

Frederick III. (1440-1493), emperor of Austria, and Maximilian I. (1493-1519).

Martin Luther (1483-1546), religious reformer.

Albert Dürer (1471-1528), painter.

Holbein (1498-1543), painter.

Copernicus (1473-1545), astronomer.

IN FRANCE.

Charles VIII. (1483-1498), king.

Rabelais (1483 or 1495-1553), satirist.

IN SPAIN.

Ferdinand (died 1516) and Isabella (died 1504), king and queen, beginning to reign in 1474.

[1]

I

THE MADONNA OF THE CHAIR

In early days an Italian in addressing a lady used the word Madonna, which, like the French word Madame, means My Lady. Now he says Signora; Madonna would have to him an old-fashioned sound. To the rest of the world this word Madonna has come to be applied almost wholly to the Virgin Mary, with or without the child Jesus; and as Raphael painted a great many pictures of the Madonna for churches or other sacred places, a name has been given to each, drawn usually from some circumstance about it.

The Madonna of the Chair is so called because in this picture the Virgin is seated. She is sitting in a low chair, holding her child on her knee, and encircling him with her arms. Her head is laid tenderly against the child's, and she looks out of the picture with a tranquil, happy sense of motherly love.

The child has the rounded limbs and playful action of the feet of a healthy, warm-blooded infant, and he nestles into his mother's embrace as snugly as a young bird in its nest. But as he leans against the mother's bosom and follows her gaze, there is a serious and even grand expression in his eyes [2] which Raphael and other painters always sought to give to the child Jesus to mark the difference between him and common children.

By the side of the Madonna is the child who is to grow up as St. John the Baptist. He carries a reed cross, as if to herald the death of the Saviour; his hands are clasped in prayer, and though the other two look out of the picture at us, he fixes his steadfast look on the child, in ardent worship.

Around each of the heads is very faintly seen a nimbus, as it is called; that is, the old painters were wont to distinguish sacred persons by a circle about the head. Sometimes, as here, the circle is a golden line only; sometimes it is a gold band almost like a plate against which the head is set. This circular form took the name Nimbus from the Latin word for a cloud, as if the heads of sacred persons were in an unearthly surrounding. It is also called a halo. Such a representation is a symbol or sign to indicate those higher and more mysterious qualities which are beyond the artist's power to portray.

This simple composition is a perfect round, and if one studies it attentively one will see how curved and flowing are all the lines within the circle; even the back of the chair, though perpendicular, swells and curves into roundness. It is by such simple means as this that the painter gives pleasure to the eye. The harmony of the lines of the composition makes a perfect expression of the peaceful group centred thus about the divine child.

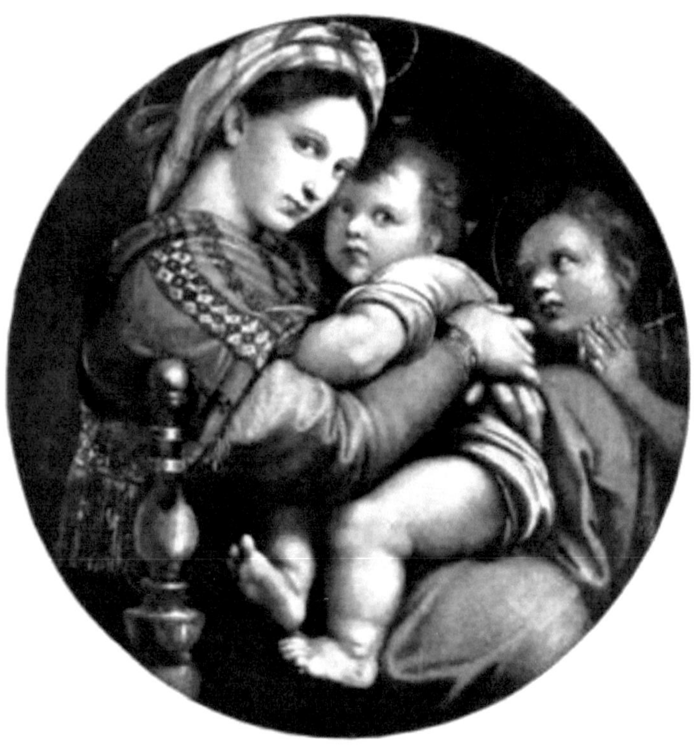

MADONNA OF THE CHAIR
Pitti Gallery, Florence

Please click on the image for a larger image.

Please click here for a modern color image

It is a home scene and one such as Raphael might [5] have seen in Rome in his own time. Not unlikely he saw a mother enfolding her child thus when he was taking a walk at the quiet end of day, and caught at once a suggestion from the scene for a Madonna. There is indeed an old legend which grew up about this picture, relating the supposed circumstances under which Raphael found a charming family group which served him as a model, and which he rapidly sketched upon the head of a cask; the circular form of the picture is thus accounted for. Whether or not this pretty story is true, it is certain that the Madonna of the Chair is a true picture of home life either in Raphael's time or even in our own day. The mother wears a handkerchief of many colors over her shoulders, and another on her head like the Roman scarf one still sees nowadays.

We may see what delight and reverence Madonna pictures like this have awakened as we read the words of an old chant. In quaint diction and with fanciful imagery the writer tried to express his feelings in the presence of a painting which, if not this veritable Madonna of the Chair, was certainly very like it.

"When I view the mother holding
In her arms the heavenly boy,
Thousand blissful thoughts unfolding
Melt my heart with sweetest joy.

"As the sun his radiance flinging
Shines upon the bright expanse,
So the child to Mary clinging
Doth her gentle heart entrance.
[6]
"See the Virgin Mother beaming!
Jesus by her arms embraced,
Dew on softest roses gleaming,
Violet with lily chaste!

"Each round other fondly twining.
Pour the shafts of mutual love,

Thick as flowers in meadow shining,
Countless as the stars above.

"Oh, may one such arrow glowing,
Sweetest Child, which thou dost dart
Thro' thy mother's bosom going,
Blessed Jesus, pierce my heart."

[7]

II

ABRAHAM AND THE THREE ANGELS

In the story of Abraham, as related in our Bible, we read of the wandering and adventurous life of the patriarch as he moved from place to place. In process of time he became "very rich in cattle, in silver, and in gold." He was as brave as he was industrious. When Lot, his brother's son, who dwelt in Sodom, was taken captive by some foreign kings who had conquered the king of Sodom, Abraham armed his large company of servants and went to the rescue. He recovered not only his nephew, but all the booty which the victors had taken. Moreover, Abraham was a man of vision as well as of action, a man who feared God and sought righteousness.

In his old age he was living with his aged wife Sarah on the plains of Mamre. "He sat in the tent door in the heat of the day," the story goes on, [1] "and he lifted up his eyes and looked, and lo, three men stood by him: and when he saw them, he ran to meet them from the tent door, and bowed himself toward the ground, and said, 'My Lord, if now I have found favour in thy sight, pass not away, I pray thee, from thy servant: let a little [8] water, I pray you, be fetched, and wash your feet, and rest yourselves under the tree: and I will fetch a morsel of bread, and comfort ye your hearts; after that ye shall pass on: for therefore are ye come to your servant.' And they said, 'So do, as thou hast said.'

[1] Genesis, chapter xviii., verses 1-8.

"And Abraham hastened into the tent unto Sarah, and said, 'Make ready quickly three measures of fine meal, knead it, and make cakes upon the hearth.' And Abraham ran unto the herd, and fetcht a calf tender and good, and gave it unto a young man; and he hasted to dress it. And he took butter, and milk, and the calf which he had dressed, and set it before them; and he stood by them under the tree, and they did eat."

In the picture we see Abraham welcoming his strange visitors in front of his simple dwelling-place. He is dressed in Oriental robes and bows himself to the ground after the custom of the Eastern people, who are noted for their courtesy. He offers hospitality not as a favor to his guests, but as a privilege which he craves from them. His, not theirs, is the honor, he seems to say.

The three angels have a mysterious air. They are in human form, and yet they are unlike ordinary visitors. Their attitudes, the flowing of the robes, their gestures, all denote something unusual. While the three stand with outstretched hands as if encouraging and blessing their host, Sarah peeps through the open door and listens to the talk. A country landscape, such as may be seen in the [11] vineyards of Italy, stretches away in the distance. Raphael never traveled outside his own country, and painted only such landscapes as were familiar to him.

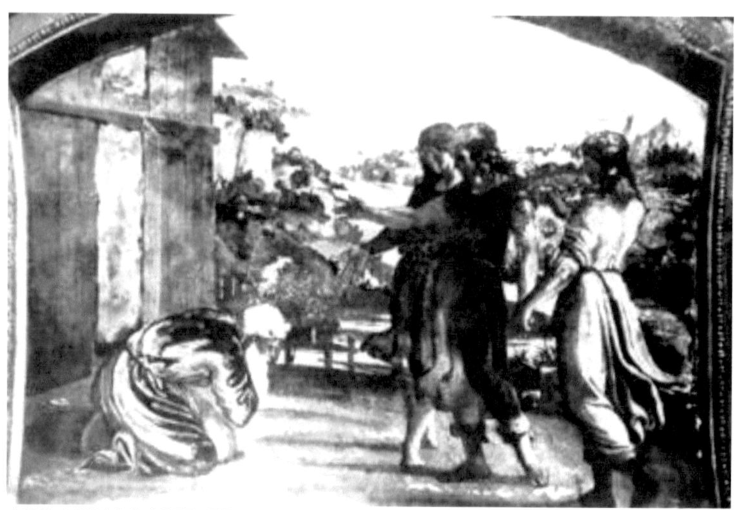

ABRAHAM AND THE THREE ANGELS
Vatican Palace, Rome

Please click on the image for a larger image.

Please click here for a modern color image

The picture was intended as an illustration of the Bible. In the days when Raphael was painting, though the art of printing had been invented, only scholars and learned men could read books, and those which were printed were rarely in the language which the people spoke. Men and women did indeed hear stories read out of the Bible, but they knew these stories chiefly from paintings, and

32

from carvings in wood and stone. Churches and monasteries, palaces and public halls, were adorned with fresco paintings, and these storied walls formed the people's literature.

Now the Pope, Leo the Tenth, employed Raphael to decorate parts of the Vatican. The Vatican was the palace of the Popes in Rome, and one of the open courts of the palace had a gallery or Loggia, as it is called, built about its three sides. Raphael caused to be painted on the walls of this gallery festoons of flowers and fruit and sometimes animals, all surrounded and entwined with graceful ornaments. But it was the vaulted ceiling of the gallery that he treated with the greatest care. He made a great series of pictures from scenes in the Old Testament, and some from the New, and his pupils painted these upon the ceiling, so that it came to be known popularly as "Raphael's Bible."

The ceiling is not flat, and it does not stretch [12] without break, but the gallery is like a succession of arched porches, and the ceiling of each is divided into panels, sloping in four directions, with a flat panel in the centre. These panels are filled with charming pictures which you can see by standing with your head thrown back.

Raphael's Bible begins with the creation of the world; then follow the history of Adam and Eve, and Noah and the deluge; in the fourth section is the story of Abraham told in four compositions. Thus, besides this picture of Abraham and the Three Angels, there is the scene where Lot and his family are fleeing from Sodom, and his wife is turned into a pillar of salt. There is also the meeting of Abraham and Melchisedec (after Abraham's rescue of Lot), and a picture of God promising a long line of descendants to Abraham.

In this open gallery the people of Rome could walk and read the Bible in a succession of pictures. Since these and similar pictures and statues and carvings were everywhere, men, women, and children read them as they would read books, and a popular painter was like a popular story-teller nowadays.

[13]

III

THE MIRACULOUS DRAUGHT OF FISHES

Another of the Bible scenes which Raphael painted was one which is told in the New Testament concerning the Lord Jesus and his Apostles. Some of these, as Peter and Andrew, James and John, were fishermen who lived near the lake of Gennesaret in Galilee, and had spent most of their lives in their boats. They had been much with their Master, and sometimes left their boats to go with him through the country, when he talked with them and healed the sick, and told the glad tidings, for that is what the word Gospel means. One day he had been using Simon Peter's boat as a sort of pulpit from which to speak to the people on the shore.

"Now when he had left speaking, he said unto Simon, 'Launch out into the deep, and let down your nets for a draught,' And Simon answering said unto him, 'Master, we have toiled all the night, and have taken nothing: nevertheless at thy word I will let down the net.' And when they had this done, they inclosed a great multitude of fishes: and their net brake. And they beckoned unto their partners, which were in the other ship, that they should come and help them. And they came, and filled both the ships, so that they began to sink. [14]

"When Simon Peter saw it, he fell down at Jesus's knees, saying, 'Depart from me: for I am a sinful man, O Lord.' For he was astonished, and all that were with him, at the draught of the fishes which they had taken; and so was also James and John, the sons of Zebedee, which were partners with Simon. And Jesus said unto Simon, 'Fear not: from henceforth thou shalt catch men.'" [2]

[2] Luke, chapter v., verses 4-10.

In the picture we see the two boats laden with fish, one containing Jesus with Peter and Andrew, and the other containing the partners hauling in the net. The lake stretches away in the distance until it seems to meet the sky in a line of light at the horizon. On the opposite shore are the people to whom Jesus was speaking before the fishermen launched out. Others on the bank are watching to get some of the fish which are not hauled in. There is a boat over there just pushing off. Fishhawks hover overhead, and on the nearer shore are herons.

Just as before in the Madonna of the Chair we saw how all the lines in the picture were drawn as it were in a circle, so here it is the long horizontal line on which the picture is built: the boats extending across the foreground, the distant shore, and the horizon line swelling into the upland. Some one has said that the boats are so placed that it looks as if the figures were slowly passing before the eye of the spectator.

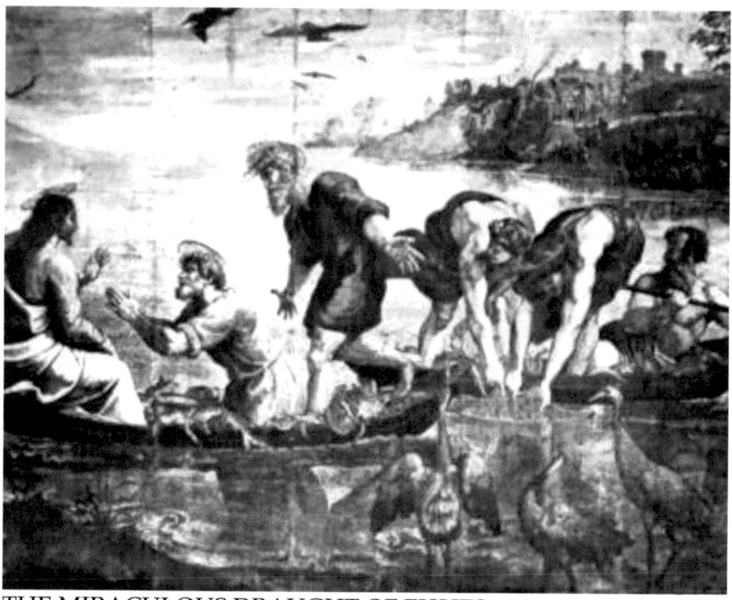

THE MIRACULOUS DRAUGHT OF FISHES
South Kensington Museum, London

Please click on the image for a larger image.

Please click here for a modern color image

Now this picture is not, like so many, painted on canvas or on wood. Raphael was bidden to make [17] designs for some great hangings or tapestries for the chapel in the Vatican palace known as the Sistine Chapel. He made his drawings, cartoons they are called, on a coarse kind of paper, the pieces put together on a great frame, and these cartoons were sent to Arras in Flanders, where they were copied in tapestry by skillful artists.

Raphael intended to represent scenes in the lives of the Apostles, and his series was in two groups of five each, the first centring about the life of St. Peter, the second about the life of St. Paul. The tapestries are in the Vatican palace, but seven of the cartoons are in the South Kensington Museum in London. There they are kept with great care, but they have led a perilous life. When they were sent to Arras, they were cut in strips for the convenience of the weavers, and pricked with holes. Then after they had been copied in the tapestries, they were thrown aside, as so much waste paper, and lay in a cellar, neglected, for a hundred years. Fortunately they were not destroyed, and the fragments were found in 1630, by the great Flemish painter Rubens, who knew their value. He advised King Charles I. of England to buy them, and they were still regarded as patterns for tapestries. The king set up a manufactory at Mortlake, and some tapestries were made from these cartoons.

When the king was put to death, Cromwell bought the cartoons, and put them away in some boxes at Whitehall. When Charles II. came to the throne, he tried to sell them to France, but was stopped, [18] and finally they found a home at Hampton Court Palace. A few years ago they were removed to their present place of keeping.

The original tapestries, as we have said, were designed for the Sistine Chapel, but they were long ago removed from that place and are now preserved in the Gallery of Tapestries in the Vatican.

The colors of the tapestries have faded, but color never formed the chief attraction of these compositions. What one always admired, and can still admire in engravings and other copies, is what we call the dramatic character of the picture, the way in which the painter has so arranged his figures as to make them tell a story in a lively, graphic fashion.

He can also, as his eye is more and more trained, discover the beauty which lies in the drawing of forms, in masses and in lines. For an engraving or a pencil drawing in black and white can give a great deal of pleasure, and some painters make better pictures with pen and ink than they can with a paint-box and brushes.

[19]

IV

THE SACRIFICE AT LYSTRA

The Sacrifice at Lystra was another of the great tapestries, and was in the second series of five which had to do with the life of St. Paul as recorded in the Acts of the Apostles. The apostle was on a journey with his companion Barnabas, and they were teaching and healing as they went. At Lystra they had performed a wonderful cure in healing a man who had been a cripple from his birth.

"And when the people saw what Paul had done, they lifted up their voices, saying in the speech of Lycaonia, 'The gods are come down to us in the likeness of men,' And they called Barnabas Jupiter, and Paul Mercurius, because he was the chief speaker.

"Then the priest of Jupiter, which was before their city, brought oxen and garlands unto the gates, and would have done sacrifice with the people. Which, when the apostles, Barnabas and Paul, heard of, they rent their clothes, and ran in among the people, crying out, and saying, 'Sirs, why do ye these things? We also are men of like passions with you, and preach unto you that ye should turn from these vanities unto the living God.' ... [20]

"And with these sayings scarce restrained they the people, that they had not done sacrifice unto them." [3]

[3] Acts of the Apostles, chapter xiv., verses 11-15, 18.

In the picture we see the two apostles standing on a platform at the left, by the steps of a temple, just as the crowd sweeps along from the other side with two oxen in the midst of them. It was just such a sacrificial procession as was formed on the days when they honored their gods in the temples. Paul and Barnabas receive the demonstration with dismay, the former rending his garments, and the latter clasping his hands in perplexity.

In the tumult of many figures we pick out five principal persons. At the right is the restored cripple whose recovery is the origin of the excitement. His folded hands, raised in adoration, come against the back of a youth who, quick to see the apostles' displeasure, reaches out an arm to stay the sacrifice. His hand nearly touches the

shoulder of the sturdy priest in front, who is lifting his axe to deal
the deathblow to the sacrificial ox. The priest's up-raised hand is
brought near the elbow of Paul, behind whom stands his fellow
apostle. Thus there is a continuous chain extending across the picture to link together those who make up the plot of the story. The
most attractive face in the company is that of the youth in the centre, eager and handsome among the stolid countenances surrounding him. The apostles themselves are presently to join him in his
efforts to restrain the people, but for the [23] moment, single-
handed among so many, he springs forward fearlessly to oppose
the purpose of the mob.

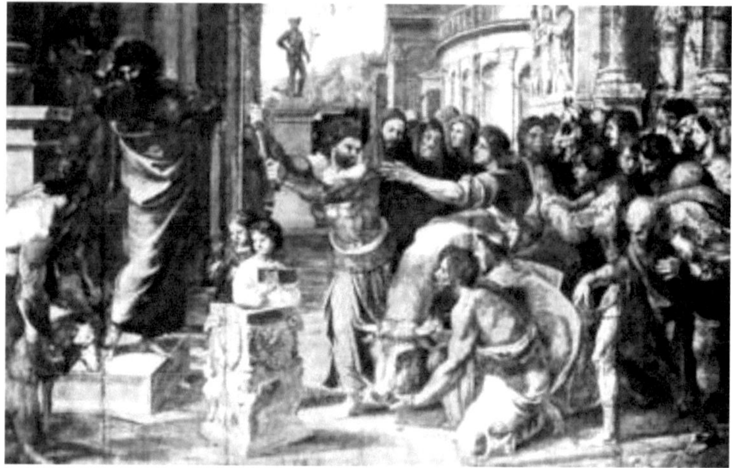

THE SACRIFICE AT LYSTRA
South Kensington Museum, London

Please click on the image for a larger image.

Please click here for a modern color image

These five figures thus linked together carry the story, but how
abundantly the scene is enriched by the minor characters! There are
not a great many figures, and each head is seen perfectly, so that
one can count the actual number of persons present; but the first
impression made on the eye is of a hurrying, eager crowd. As one
looks more closely, he discovers particular persons who help to fill
out the story. There are two priestesses kneeling beside the ox that

is to be sacrificed. One figure, other than the cripple who has been healed, is shown in the attitude of prayer. Perhaps the old man at the extreme right is drawing aside the robe of the cripple, curious to see if there are any signs of the miracle, or if that really was the leg which was helpless.

The two children who stand by the altar, one playing the pipes, the other with a book of music, are very characteristic of Raphael, who loved thus to introduce a playful, innocent element. The singing child has his eyes bent on the ram which is led up for sacrifice.

Raphael, like other illustrators of the Bible, does not always follow exactly the text which he is to illustrate. The people called Barnabas Jupiter, and Paul Mercury. This would seem to show that Barnabas was a great, imposing figure, and Paul, according to tradition, was a small, undersized man; but there is no such contrast to be seen here. [24]

By a happy suggestion, the painter has placed in the background on a pedestal a statue of Mercury. We know it by the winged staff which Mercury is supposed to carry as a sign of his office of messenger of the gods.

Raphael painted at a time when scholars and artists were enthusiastic over the rediscovery of the literature and art of the ancient world. Such a scene as this, therefore, appealed to him; for he could not only depict a Biblical incident, but he could make his picture a study of ancient life. The architecture, the altar, the figure of Mercury, the wreath-bound heads, the sacrificial act itself, were all such as he could imagine from ancient Greece. Indeed, the whole picture is like a copy of an antique bas-relief; and in the original cartoon there is, below the picture, a decorative border studied from antique sculpture, and below that still an ornamental edge which was very common in Greek work.

And yet, though Raphael thus made much of the Greek spirit in his design, he was like all great painters of his day. He did not try minutely to repeat Greek life as he imagined it. The men and women and children were like those he was wont to see in Rome or Florence, or Urbino, where he was born, and the headdresses were such as the women of his time wore.

[25]

V

HELIODORUS DRIVEN FROM THE TEMPLE

In the Vatican palace there is one chamber in a series of chambers decorated with Raphael's paintings which is called in Italian Stanza d'Eliodoro, or the Heliodorus Room. The name is taken from the first of the paintings which cover the walls of the room.

The story which Raphael told in this picture is taken from an incident in the history of Jerusalem, which is related in one of the books of the Apocrypha and in Josephus's History.

It was at a time when Jerusalem was a prosperous city, owing its good government to the upright and honorable character of the high priest Onias. Through his efforts a large fund of money and treasure had been laid up for the relief of widows and orphans. This treasure was stored in the sacred precincts of the temple and carefully guarded for the uses for which it was intended.

Now it came about that a distant king heard of this valuable treasure and set his heart upon it. He called his treasurer Heliodorus, and straightway sent him to Jerusalem to bring back the treasure by fair means or foul. Heliodorus was a bold man ready for his evil task. Arriving at Jerusalem, he sought [26] out Onias and made his demand, which, as a matter of course, was promptly refused. Heliodorus then prepared to take the treasure by force, and, accompanied by his men, pushed into the temple amid the lamentations of the people and the prayers of the priests. But just as the robbers had laid hands upon the coveted treasure, a strange thing happened; and this is what the old narrative relates: —

"There appeared unto them a horse with a terrible rider upon him, and adorned with a very fair covering, and he ran fiercely and smote at Heliodorus with his forefeet, and it seemed that he that sat upon the horse had complete harness of gold.

"Moreover, two other young men appeared before him, notable in strength, excellent in beauty, and comely in apparel, who stood by him on either side, and scourged him continually and gave him many sore stripes.

"And Heliodorus fell suddenly unto the ground, and was compassed with great darkness." [4]

[4] Maccabees, book ii., chapter iii., verses 25-27.

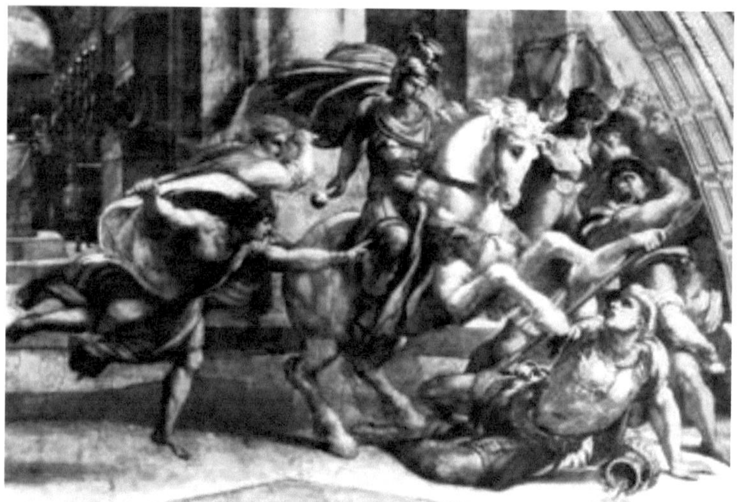

HELIODORUS DRIVEN FROM THE TEMPLE
Vatican Palace, Rome

Please click on the image for a larger image.

Please click here for a modern color image

In the picture the priests still kneel at the distant altar while the temple treasures are being borne away in heavy chests and jars. Meanwhile swift retribution overtakes the despoiler. In gallops the mysterious gold-armored horseman, his prancing steed crushing the prostrate Heliodorus under his forefeet. On rush the two celestial avengers, springing through the air in great flying leaps. Their feet do not touch the ground as, with outspread arms and wind-blown hair, they bound lightly forward, [29] raising their scourges to drive out the enemy. Heliodorus vainly lifts his spear to save himself; his men are panic-stricken; his plot is undone. And yet in all this the angelic avengers do not touch one of the prostrate or falling figures. Even the horse's hoofs are not planted on Heliodorus. The victory is not won by force, but by the mysterious power of celestial spirits.

Here is the way this picture affected a lover of art who stood before it: "The Scourging of Heliodorus is full of energy, power, and movement. The horse and his rider are irresistible, and the scourging youths, terrible as embodied lightning; mortal weapons and mortal muscles are powerless as infancy before such supernatural energies. Like flax before the flame—like leaves before the storm— the strong man and his attendants are consumed and borne away."

There is an interesting contrast in this great picture, for while all this terrible action is going on at one side, one sees in an opposite part a group of women and children, looking on with astonishment and alarm. Near by is a figure carried in a chair on the shoulders of strong men. This figure is Pope Julius II, and the reason why Raphael introduced him into the painting is as follows:—

Julius was a warlike Pope who had expelled the enemies of the church from the Papal territories and enlarged the boundaries of these territories. He was also a great patron of the arts. He called on Raphael to make designs for this chamber which [30] should represent the miraculous deliverance of the church from her secular foes; and as he was regarded as the chief instrument in the victory, Raphael made him present at this Expulsion of Heliodorus.

Not only the walls of the Heliodorus Room are adorned with pictures, but the ceiling also is covered with designs, illustrating four Old Testament stories of divine promises to the patriarchs: The Promise of God to Abraham of a numerous posterity, [5] The Sacrifice of Isaac, Jacob's Dream, Moses and the Burning Bush.

[5] Sometimes interpreted as God appearing to Noah.

Probably Raphael, who had friends among the cardinals and other learned men of Rome, consulted them as to the selection of subjects for this room. One can trace the thought which binds them all together. On the ceiling we have God's promises made to his people of old, while the pictures on the walls show how the same watchful Providence delivered the church in later years.

[31]

VI

THE LIBERATION OF PETER

On the wall below the design of Jacob's Dream, in the ceiling of this same Heliodorus Room, is the Liberation of Peter, painted above and on each side of a window. The story is taken from the Acts of the Apostles, Herod the king, as the narrative says, "stretched forth his hands to vex certain of the church. And he killed James the brother of John with the sword. And because he saw it pleased the Jews, he proceeded further to take Peter also." The story of the imprisonment and liberation of Peter now follows: —

"And when he had apprehended him, he put him in prison, and delivered him to four quarternions of soldiers to keep him; intending after Easter to bring him forth to the people. Peter therefore was kept in prison; but prayer was made without ceasing of the church unto God for him.

"And when Herod would have brought him forth, the same night Peter was sleeping between two soldiers, bound with two chains; and the keepers before the door kept the prison. And behold, the angel of the Lord came upon him, and a light shined in the prison; and he smote Peter on the side, and raised him up, saying, 'Arise up quickly.' And his [32] chains fell off from his hands. And the angel said unto him, 'Gird thyself, and bind on thy sandals.' And so he did. And he saith unto him, 'Cast thy garment about thee, and follow me.' And he went out, and followed him, and wist not that it was true which was done by the angel; but thought he saw a vision." [6]

[6] Acts of the Apostles, chapter xii., verses 4-9.

There is a succession of scenes in this story, and as the window runs up into the wall, it gave Raphael an opportunity to distribute the successive incidents in the three divisions thus formed. Over the window, accordingly, is the scene of the awakening of Peter. The angel, surrounded by a blaze of light, comes and smites the sleeping apostle on the side, but his action also indicates that he raises him and points to the door. Peter is shown bound by two chains, each fastening him to one of the soldiers, who are both asleep at their posts. The bars through which we see the scene are the prison bars.

At the right of the window, the angel is shown leading Peter past the guards, who are asleep on the steps. The prison is indicated by the thick wall and solid masonry, by the side of which the two figures are passing. The soldiers by their attitude show how sound asleep they are, — one stretched out at half length, trying to look as if he were awake, the other with his head fallen forward, and his hands clasped over his shield.

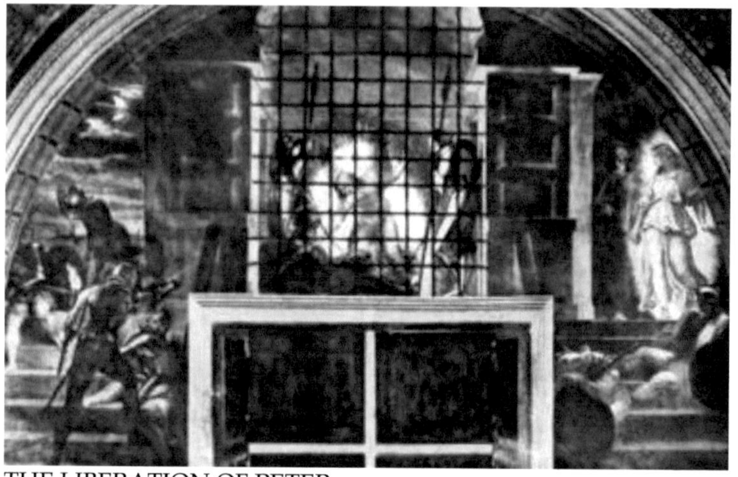

THE LIBERATION OF PETER
Vatican Palace, Rome

Please click on the image for a larger image.

Please click here for a modern color image

In both of these scenes, the apostle is marked by the sign of the nimbus, which we saw in the first [35] picture, the Madonna of the Chair. But if you look narrowly, you will see that Raphael has added that other sign by which Peter is distinguished. He carries a great key. The reason is to be found in the words of our Lord to him as recorded in the Gospel of Matthew, the sixteenth chapter and nineteenth verse. The key is a most fitting symbol here, for it seems to imply that the apostle is himself opening the gates of his prison house. The angel holds his hand, as an older person might lead a child in the dark. Peter is too dazed to know what has really happened.

On the left is depicted the moment when the guards are awakened and discover that their prisoner has escaped. It is an animated scene illustrating the simple words of the gospel narrative: "Now as soon as it was day, there was no small stir among the soldiers, what was become of Peter." A man with a torch tells by his gesture that something extraordinary has happened, and the one whom he arouses shows by his face and his uplifted hand how startled he is; the light from the torch is too dazzling for another just awakened, and the last of all appears to be the one whom we saw asleep over his shield.

Even in this very inadequate copy of a great painting, we can see what is the noblest and most pervading beauty. It is the treatment of light. The angel appears in the compartment over the window in a blaze of light, and this light illuminates all the other figures. So it is in the right-hand [36] division, and Peter especially shows it, for the side away from the angel is scarcely to be made out in the gloom. In the left-hand division, the torch, the moon struggling through the clouds, and the breaking of the dawn diffuse a light over the whole scene.

It is as if Raphael meant to make it clear that the supernatural light from the angel was brighter and more intense than the light which falls from natural means. Thus the Liberation of Peter, like the Expulsion of Heliodorus, keeps in mind the power of the divine over the human. Some have thought, besides, that Raphael had in his thought the recent delivery from captivity of Leo X., the Pope who succeeded Pope Julius II., for the decoration of the Heliodorus Room was done successively under these two popes.

[37]

VII

THE HOLY FAMILY OF FRANCIS I

There are a great many pictures by the old masters representing what is known as the Holy Family. This is a group consisting of the mother and child, with one or more additional figures. The third figure is sometimes the infant John the Baptist, or it may be Joseph the husband of Mary; a fourth figure is likely to be St. Elizabeth, the mother of John the Baptist, and sometimes all five of these are shown in a group.

That is the case with the painting of The Holy Family by Raphael, which is now in the Louvre gallery in Paris, and is called The Holy Family of Francis the First, because Raphael painted the picture for that king of France. It is not difficult to make out the several figures, for the painter has followed the natural order.

The light falls chiefly on the child Jesus, who is springing up, as Mary lifts him from his cradle. His happy, joyous face is raised with a glad smile to the down-glancing mother. She has eyes only for him, and into her face there has come a look of sweet gravity which helps one to see that this is more than the play of a mother and child.

Eagerly reaching forward to the golden-haired [38] Jesus is the swarthy John the Baptist, his hands folded in the gesture of prayer, the cross which he carries as the herald of Jesus leaning against his breast, and a look of bright wonder in his face.

Leaning over and holding him is his mother, Elizabeth, whom the great painters were wont to figure as an old woman, after the description of her in the gospel as "well stricken in years." She also gazes down at her child with a like expression of deep feeling, as if she always carried about in her mind the wonderful scenes which attended his birth.

Behind the group is Joseph, the husband of Mary, in an attitude which is very common in the old pictures. He rarely seems to be a part of the group. He stands a little way off looking on, with a thoughtful air, as if he were the guardian of this pair. Sometimes he is shown with a staff or crutch, and it may be that here he rests his elbow on it, while his head leans upon his half-closed hand.

All these are distinguished by the nimbus which encircles the head of a sacred person, but the two other figures in the picture have no nimbus, for they are angels, as may be seen by the out-stretched wing of one of them, and by the pure unearthly expression on their faces. One of these angels strews flowers over the child; the other, with hands crossed on the breast, is rapt in adoration.

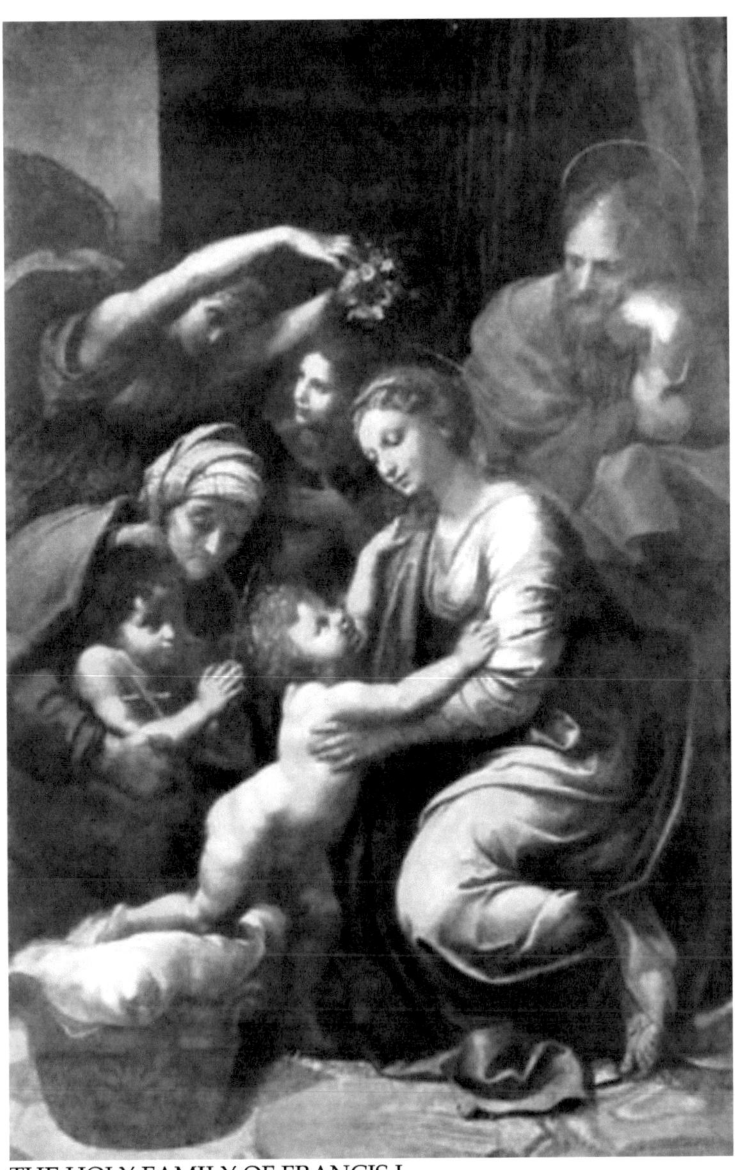

THE HOLY FAMILY OF FRANCIS I.
The Louvre, Paris

Please click on the image for a larger image.

Please click here for a modern color image

There is an opening which shows the sky, and it almost seems as if the angels with crossed hands were listening to some divine melody that came in with the angelic visitors. The whole scene is bathed [41] in light, and the longer we look the more we see the beauty of the lines which flow in the picture as if to some heavenly music. All is action save in the grave, contemplative figure of Joseph; and his serious, resting attitude by its contrast makes more evident the leaping child, the mother half stooping to lift him, John the Baptist pressing forward and Elizabeth gently restraining him, with the two flying, radiant angels.

The power which a great painting has over us often makes us ask, How did the painter do this? did he think of everything beforehand? did he paint the picture bit by bit, or did he rapidly sketch it all as he meant to have it, and then at leisure fill in the parts, and add this or that?

We know something of how painters work, and of the labor which they sometimes put into their pictures, rubbing out and painting over. A great master like Raphael always gives a sense of ease to his work, as though it cost him nothing. But we know also that he took the greatest pains as he took the greatest delight in his work.

It happens that there exist drawings made by Raphael when he was preparing to paint this very picture, and it is interesting to see how he went to work. He has a young woman in his studio take just the attitude which a mother would take who was about to lift her child. That he may be sure to draw the form correctly, he has her dress not fall below her knee, and she has bare arms. In this way he will know just how the arm and the knee will [42] bend, and how the muscles will show. Then he makes another drawing with the dress falling to the ground, but with the arm bare. Finally he draws the arm with the sleeve over it.

It was by such studies that he made sure of drawing correctly. They are like exercises in grammar. But when he came to paint his picture, he had not to think much about the correctness of his draw-

54

ing; his whole mind was intent upon making his peasant girl look as he imagined the Virgin Mary to look.

[43]

VIII

ST. CATHERINE OF ALEXANDRIA

This is the legend of St. Catherine.

She was the daughter of King Costis and his wife Sabinella, who was herself the daughter of the king of Egypt. When she came into the world, a glory of light was seen to play around her head, and when she was yet a little child, she gave such signs of wisdom that she was a wonder to all about the court of Egypt. When she was no more than fourteen years old, she was a marvel of learning. She could have answered all the hard questions the Queen of Sheba asked Solomon, and she knew her Plato by heart.

At this time her father died, and so Catherine became queen; but this did not change her way of living. She read her books and shut herself up in the palace to study. Now this did not please her nobles, and they besought her to take a husband who should help her rule the people, and who should lead them in war. At this the girl asked them:—

"What manner of man is this that I must marry?" And one of the nobles made answer:—

"Madam, you are our sovereign lady and queen, and all the world knows that you have four notable gifts. First, you are come of the most noble blood [44] in the whole world; second, you have a great inheritance in your kingdom; third, you surpass all persons living in knowledge; and fourth, you are most beautiful. So, then, you must needs take a husband that you may have an heir who shall be the comfort and joy of your people."

"Is it indeed so?" said the young queen. "Then, if God has given me such gifts, I am the more bound to love him and please him, and set small store by my wisdom and beauty and riches and birth. He that shall be my husband must also possess four notable gifts. He must be of so noble blood, that all men shall worship him, and so great that I shall never think I have made him king; so rich, that he will surpass all others in riches; so full of beauty, that the angels of God will desire to behold him; and so benign, that he will gladly forgive all wrong done unto him. Find me such an one, and I will make him lord of my heart."

Now there was a certain hermit who dwelt in the desert about two days' journey from Alexandria, and the Virgin Mary appeared to him and bade him go and tell Catherine to fear not, for she should have a heavenly bridegroom, even her Son, who was greater than any monarch of the world, being himself the King of Glory, and the Lord of all power.

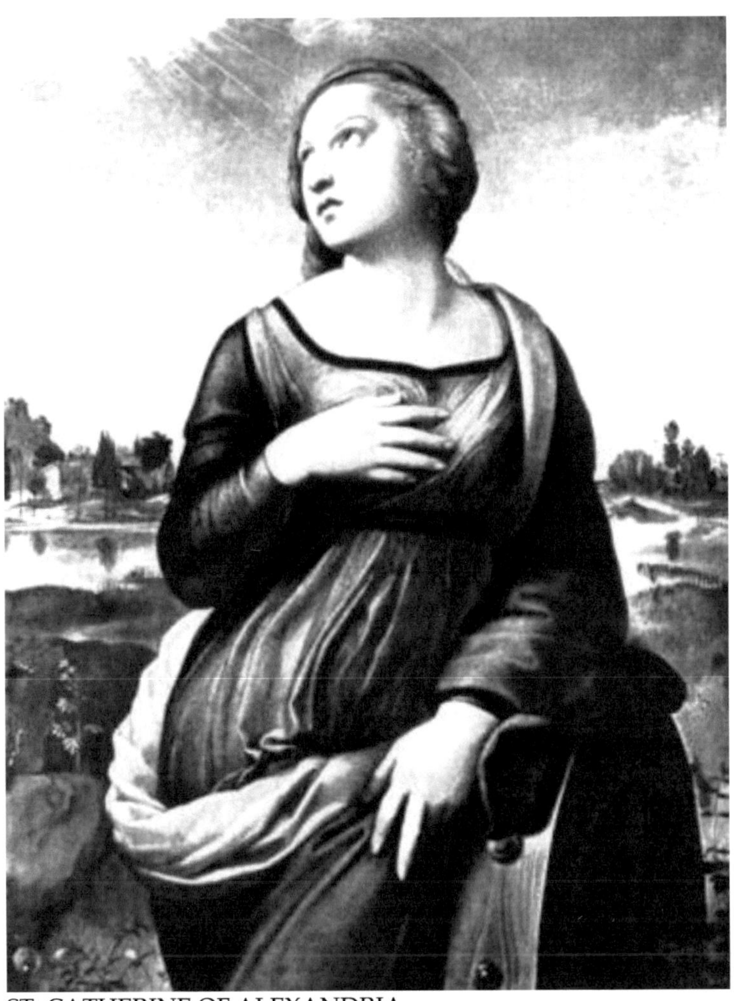

ST. CATHERINE OF ALEXANDRIA
National Gallery, London

Please click on the image for a larger image.

Please click here for a modern color image

Until now the young queen had been a heathen, but when the hermit showed her a picture of the Lord Christ, she was so filled with wonder and devotion that she forgot her books and her learning and could think only of him. And thus it came about [47] that she had a strange dream, in which she dreamt that she was brought to the Lord, and he said, "She is not fair or beautiful enough for me."

She woke in tears and sent for the hermit, who came and taught her the Christian faith. She was baptized and her mother Sabinella with her. Again she had a dream, and this time the Lord smiled on her, and put a ring on her finger.

So now Catherine despised still more earthly pomp and riches, and being thus plighted to a heavenly bridegroom, she refused more steadfastly all the attempts of her nobles to persuade her to be married. The good Sabinella sustained her in this, but at last died, and Catherine was now left alone.

Then came the great emperor Maximin, who persecuted the Christians. And he came to Alexandria and called the Christians together, and commanded them, on pain of torment, to worship the heathen gods. When Queen Catherine heard the uproar, she came forth of the palace and stood before Maximin. She so used her learning, that she silenced the emperor, and he could make no reply.

Thereupon he ordered fifty of his most famous wise men to dispute with her. But she answered them so convincingly that they themselves became Christians, and Maximin was in such a rage that he burned them to death, yet they did not flinch.

Then did the emperor drag Catherine from her palace and cast her into a dungeon. But the faithful queen prayed, and angels came and ministered to her. At the end of twelve days the empress [48] came to visit her, and found the dungeon filled with light and fragrant with sweet odors. So she and two hundred of her attendants fell down at the feet of Catherine and declared themselves Christians.

When Maximin found what had taken place he was filled with fury, and put to death the empress and all the converts. But he was so overcome with the beauty of Catherine that he offered to make her empress if she would forsake Christ.

When Catherine exclaimed: "Shall I forsake my glorious heavenly bridegroom to unite myself with thee, who art base-born, wicked, and deformed?" Then Maximin bade his men make four wheels, armed with sharp points and blades, two turning in one direction, two in another, so that the tender body of the beautiful queen should be torn asunder.

So they bound her between the wheels, and at the same moment fire came down from heaven, and the destroying angel broke the wheels in pieces, which flew off and killed the executioner.

Then Maximin, with his heart of stone, commanded that Catherine be carried outside the city, and scourged and then beheaded. So it was done; but when she was dead, angels bore her body over the desert and over the Red Sea, and laid it away on the top of Mt. Sinai. As for the tyrant, he was slain in battle, and the vultures devoured him.

In our picture of St. Catherine, and in others like it, she is shown standing by a wheel. She leans upon it as if ready for martyrdom, and looks upward as if she saw the fire coming down from heaven.

[49]

IX

ST. CECILIA

The legend of St. Cecilia is not so tragic as that of St. Catherine. According to the story, Cecilia was a beautiful young girl who belonged to a noble Roman family of the third century.

Her parents were Christians in secret, and they brought her up in the faith. She was a most devout scholar. Night and day she carried about with her a roll containing the Gospel, hidden within her robe. She excelled in music, and turned her good gift to the glory of God; for she composed hymns which she sang with such sweetness, that it was said the very angels descended from heaven to join their voices with hers.

Not only did she sing, but she played also on all instruments; but she could find none which satisfied her desire to breathe forth the harmony which dwelt within her, and so she invented a new one, the forerunner of the organ, and she consecrated it to the service of God.

St. Cecilia like St. Catherine was a martyr, but the executioner who was to put her to death was so affected by her innocence that his hand trembled, and the wounds he made did not immediately cause her death. She lived for three days, and as the story says: [50]

—

"She spent (these days) in prayers and exhortations to the converts, distributing to the poor all she possessed; and she called to her St. Urban, and desired that her house, in which she then lay dying, should be converted into a place of worship for the Christians. Thus, full of faith and charity, and singing with her sweet voice praises and hymns to the last moment, she died at the end of three days."

Very naturally, St. Cecilia was taken as the patron saint of musicians, and is sometimes represented as seated at a modern organ. In this picture she is shown holding in her hands an instrument of reeds, which may be taken as the beginning of the organ of later days.

Her eyes are raised, and her head is upturned as she listens to the choir of angels shown above in the clouds, their lips parted as they sing from open books. She holds the instrument, but she is so intent on the music she hears that it seems almost slipping from her hands.

Indeed, some of the tubes are already dropping out of their place; and as the eye follows them, it rests upon a number of other musical instruments lying on the ground, — the pipe, the violin, the tambourine, castanets, and others. It is as if we were shown the various instruments which she had set aside as not satisfying to her, and at last were shown her organ itself falling to pieces and dropping from her hands. So faint and imperfect, the painter seems to say, are all these forms of earthly music when compared with the heavenly.

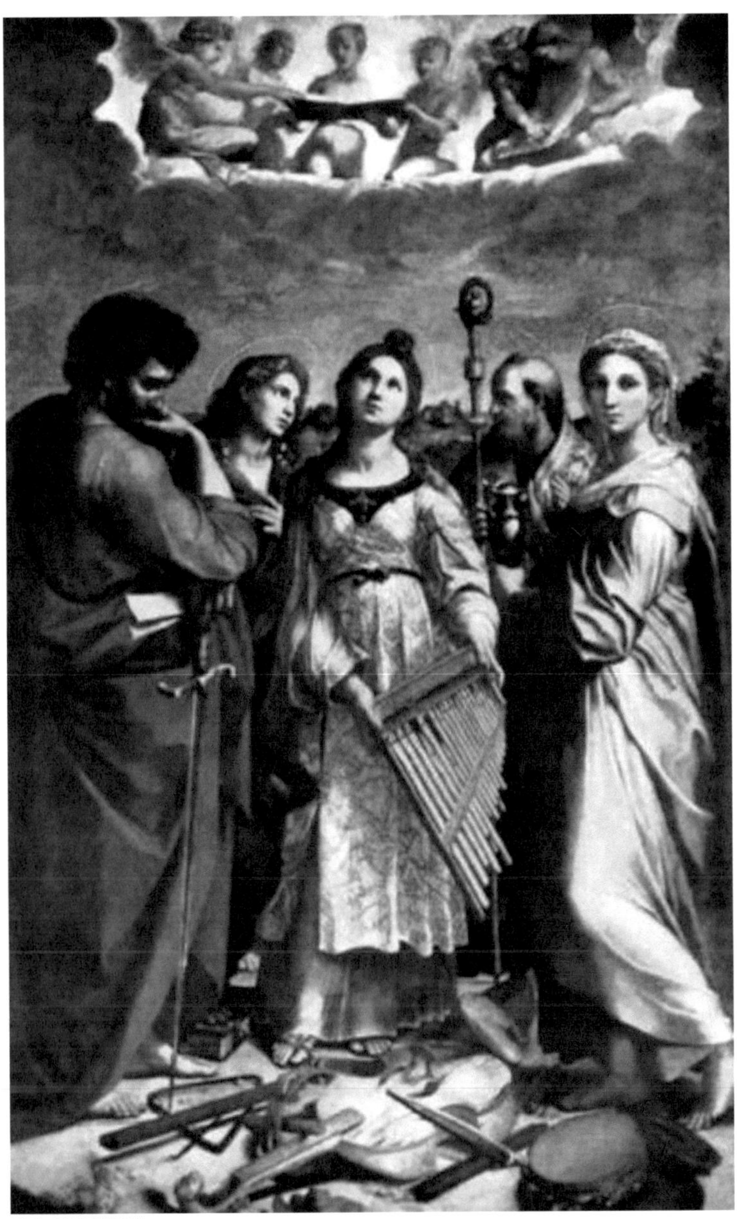

ST. CECILIA

Bologna Gallery

Please click on the image for a larger image.

Please click here for a modern color image

[53]

St. Cecilia is here in a company of other saints, not indeed of her day and generation, but chosen by Raphael to give expression to various ideas and sentiments. St. Paul, the great apostle to the Gentiles, stands in a thoughtful attitude, one hand carrying a scroll and resting on the hilt of a sword; for in one of his epistles, he speaks of "the sword of the Spirit, which is the word of God." He is listening, and at the same time looks down upon the instruments as if he were thinking how his earthly words, too, were dull beside the voice of the Spirit.

On the opposite side of the picture is Mary Magdalene. She holds the pot of ointment with which she anointed the feet of Christ, and by the movement of her feet she seems just to have come into the scene, and looks out of the picture as if she were bidding us and all other spectators look on the saint and listen to the angels. Perhaps the artist, in choosing her for one of his figures, was mindful of the words of the Lord, who praised her for bringing a precious gift, without thinking of its worth, simply because she loved him, and wished to show her devotion. So St. Cecilia poured out her music, the richest gift she had, not thinking how she could turn it into money and give it to the poor.

Next to St. Paul, behind him and St. Cecilia, stands the evangelist St. John. Painters and scholars alike have always seen in this figure the beloved disciple, the one who leaned on the Lord's breast at the last supper, and they delight to show him as a young man of refined and beautiful coun [54] tenance. His hand, with the parted fingers, seems to make a gesture bidding one listen, and his face has a look of rapture. It was natural indeed that Raphael should thus have placed in the company one whose gospel is full of feeling, the life of Christ set to music as it were.

Finally, we have St. Augustine, one of the Fathers of the church, standing in his priestly robe and holding a bishop's crook. He is apparently exchanging glances with St. John. Perhaps he is designed to show that the church makes much of music in its service.

If we could see the painting itself with its beautiful color, we should see even more distinctly not only how Raphael thought out his design, making his figures all have a harmonious relation to one another, but how perfectly the composition, in its lines, its light and color, expresses this musical harmony of heaven and earth.

[55]

X

THE TRANSFIGURATION

The Transfiguration is a picture divided into two parts. The lower part is filled with more figures than the upper and contains more action. On one side are nine of the disciples of Jesus; on the other is a crowd of people in company with a father who brings his son to be healed. He gives an account of his boy's sickness in these words: —

"He is mine only child. And lo! a spirit taketh him, and he suddenly crieth out; and it teareth him that he foameth again; and, bruising him, hardly departeth from him." [7]

[7] Luke, chapter ix., verses 38, 39.

The father calls upon the disciples, in the absence of Jesus, to heal his son. In the company with him, we can make out two women kneeling by the boy. We think it is the mother who supports him, and looks at the disciples as she points to her son. How quiet and self-possessed she is, in contrast to the poor fellow's violence as shown in his position, and his distorted hands.

She is wholly devoted to him, and the mother shows in her face and bearing. But the other kneeling woman, who may be his sister, carries a different expression as she points to the boy. She looks [56] toward the disciples with a severe and scornful air, as if saying: "What! you profess to heal the sick, and you can do nothing for this poor sufferer!"

The figures in the background are crying aloud and stretching out their arms for aid. One can count the persons, but it looks as if there were a crowd behind that we do not see, all pressing forward.

On the other side of the picture are the disciples, all eager, with heads bent forward, and each gesturing to express his meaning. One, younger than the others, with his hand against his breast, looks at the father with a pitying but helpless expression, as if he would gladly help him if he only could. Another has an open book as though he were trying to find some word of comfort. One is pointing out the boy to his neighbor, and two in the background seem to be lost in perplexity.

But, after all, though most of the disciples are thus intent, the eye quickly notes the action of a figure near the centre, full of fire and energy, who is pointing upward, away from the group, and calling upon the father and the women to look that way. And the line of his arm thrust out is continued by that of another disciple behind him, who also points upward.

For these two have seen the Lord, and they are bidding the troubled parents look the same way for help. There, above all this turmoil and confusion, is a scene of dazzling light, of which they alone seem to be aware.

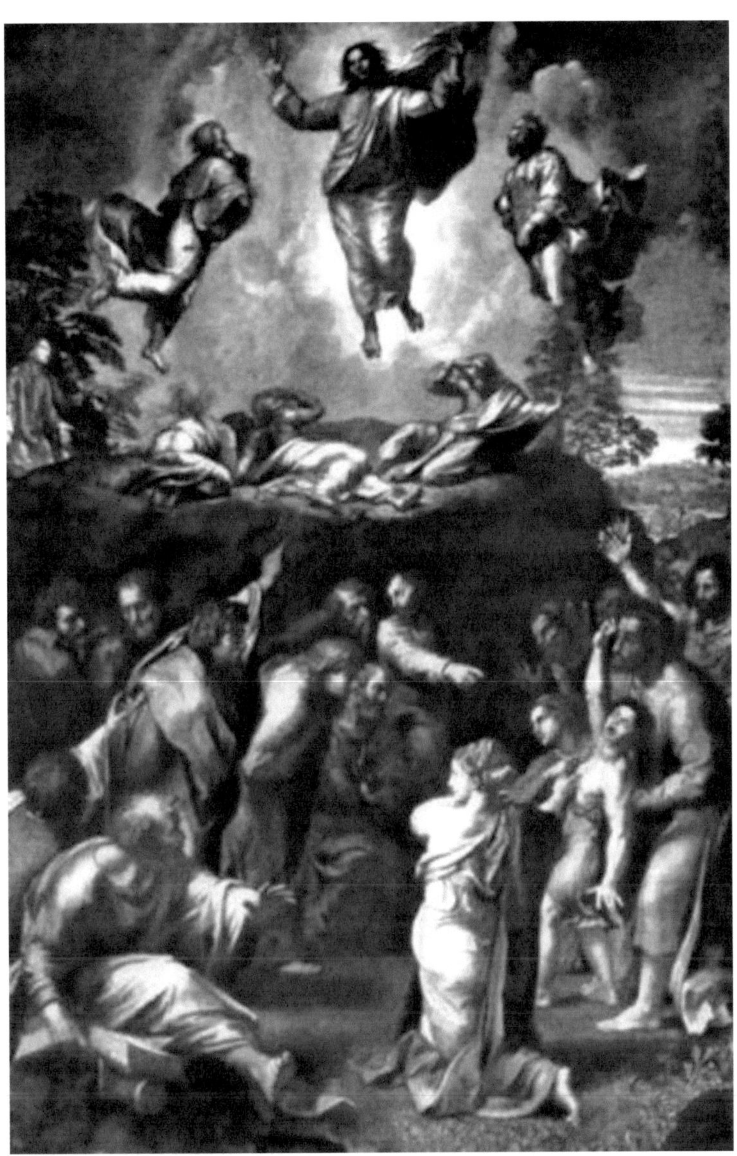

THE TRANSFIGURATION
Vatican Gallery, Rome

Please click on the image for a larger image.

Please click here for a modern color image

[59]

The upper part of the picture discloses the transfiguration of the Saviour. As the evangelist tells us, he had taken Peter and James and John with him, and had gone up into a mountain to pray.

"And as he prayed, the fashion of his countenance was altered, and his raiment was white and glistering. And, behold, there talked with him two men, which were Moses and Elias, who appeared in glory, and spake of his decease which he should accomplish at Jerusalem. But Peter and they that were with him were heavy with sleep; and when they were awake, they saw his glory, and the two men that stood with him." [8]

[8] Luke, chapter ix., verses 29-32.

The scene shown is at the moment of the awaking of the three disciples, one not daring to look up again, but bowing his head and folding his hands in prayer. They are dazzled with the glory. This glory is a cloud of brightness which envelops the three figures of Christ, Moses, and Elijah, or as the Greeks called him, Elias. The Saviour looks heavenward with rapture in his gaze.

On one side are seen two kneeling figures. They are said to stand for the father and uncle of the Cardinal who ordered the picture from Raphael. It was the fashion of the day thus to introduce a patron into a painting, and Raphael has made them as obscure as he well could.

We must not look at this great picture as if it were a panorama, where a succession of scenes is witnessed, or find fault with it because the Bible [60] says that the transfiguration took place on one day and the scene below took place the next day, when Jesus and his disciples had come down from the mountain. Nor is anything said in the Bible which would lead us to suppose that Jesus and the prophets were raised above the ground.

No; what Raphael intended was to draw a contrast between an earthly scene of suffering and a heavenly scene of peace and serenity; and he took two scenes which lie next each other in the scripture narrative. That was his thought, and see how wonderfully he has expressed this contrast throughout!

There is the dark confusion and helplessness and grief below; above is a scene of light which is like a vision, and this vision two of the disciples see; and as we have pointed out, a contrast is made evident in various parts of the picture. Indeed, the painting is made up of contrasts; and not the least noticeable is that of the solid mass below, square shaped, and the light, pyramid-shaped composition above.

The Transfiguration was the last painting to which Raphael set his brush, and it was still unfinished when he was suddenly stricken with fever and died. As his body lay in state, in the hall where he had been working, this great picture was hung at the head, and the people who came in fell to weeping when they saw it.

[63]

XI

PARNASSUS

Raphael was but twenty-five years old when he was bidden adorn a room in the Vatican palace, and he made the four walls answer to four divisions in the ceiling, just as afterward in the Heliodorus room. The four divisions in the ceiling were filled with four figures, representing Theology, Poetry, Philosophy, and Justice. Beneath Poetry was this large, full design of Parnassus.

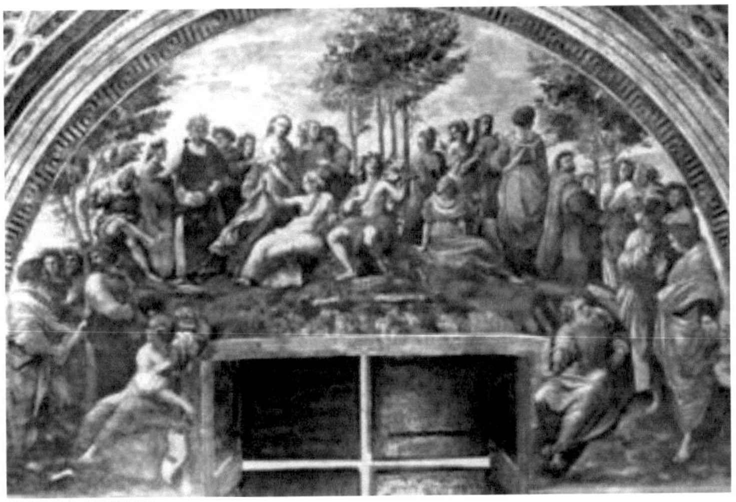

PARNASSUS
Vatican Palace, Rome

Please click on the image for a larger image.

Please click here for a modern color image

Parnassus, in the old Greek myth, was the mountain on which the muses were wont to meet, and here Apollo had his chief seat. Here, in the fancy of the ancients, the poets and historians and dramatists came to draw inspiration. So Raphael has made a great company of gods and goddesses, and ancient and modern poets.

By means of the accompanying diagram, all the figures in the composition can be made out.

As it is an imaginary scene, Raphael was free to bring together poets of different ages and countries, grouping them by the natural association of one with another. In this mythic realm time and space are as nothing, and the poets are united in the higher fellowship of the inspired imagination.

[64]

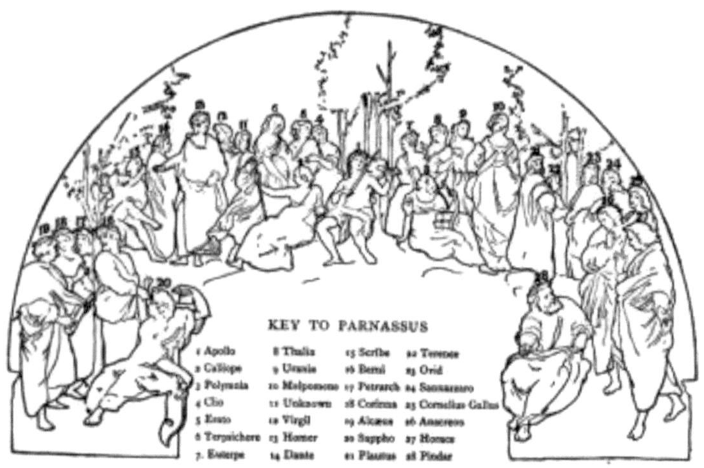

KEY TO PARNASSUS
1. Apollo 2. Calliope 3. Polymnia 4. Clio 5. Erato 6. Terpsichore 7. Euterpe 8. Thalia 9. Urania 10. Melpomene 11. Unknown 12. Virgil 13. Homer 14. Dante 15. Scribe 16. Berni 17. Petrarch 18. Corinna 19. Alcæus 20. Sappho 21. Plautus 22. Terence 23. Ovid 24. Sannazzaro 25. Cornelius Gallus 26. Anacreon 27. Horace 28. Pindar

Please click on the image for a larger image.

[65]

It is interesting to note how the painter has brought them together. Apollo, of course, as the god of poetry and music, occupies the central position, seated beneath some laurel trees, near the sacred fountain of Hippocrene, with the nine Muses circling about him. Apollo is always spoken of as playing the lyre, but Raphael gives him a violin, because the action in playing that instrument is so graceful. Some think also he meant to pay a compliment to a famous violinist of that day.

Calliope, the muse of epic poetry, rests for a moment the long trumpet whose epic strains are wont to stir the courage of men. Polymnia, the muse of sacred poetry, leans upon the lyre whose vibrant strings thrill the gentler emotions of faith and love.

Blind old Homer advances chanting the adventures of the Greek heroes, and an eager youth writes down the verses. Behind him are Virgil and Dante, and Virgil seems to be calling on Dante to listen to Apollo.

Another group shows Pindar, a very aged figure, reciting his impassioned odes to Horace and another poet, who listen with admiration. Plautus and Terence, two writers of Latin comedy, walk together in pleasant companionship.

It was not an easy matter to dispose of the many figures and groups in a space cut into, as this wall is, by a window, but how free and how natural is the arrangement! It was among the first great paintings which Raphael executed in the Vatican, and the grace and harmony which mark his later works are here shown. [66]

The picture is interesting also as another illustration of the great revival of learning which took place in Raphael's day. The old literature of Greece and Rome had been rediscovered. For centuries it had lain like a buried city, forgotten under the ignorance and the fighting of the Middle Ages. Now it was brought to light, and the recovered treasure was the common possession of Italy, not indeed so much of the plain people as of the learned men and the artists.

Raphael, as an artist, took delight in the statues which had been found, and the other signs of Greek and Roman art; but it is not to be supposed that he would know Homer and Virgil and Horace and Pindar and Sappho at first hand. He had, however, friends among the learned men, who could tell him of the treasures of classic literature, and his imagination was quick to seize this material and adapt it to artistic purposes.

Note.—The key to Parnassus on page 61 is based on the description of the painting in Cav. E. G. Massi's "Descrizione delle Gallerie di Pittura nel Pontificio Palazzo Vaticano," the authoritative guidebook to the Vatican. Miss Eliza Allen Starr, in her monograph on the frescoes of the Camera della Segnatura, called "The Three Keys," identifies some of the figures differently, following the authority of Dandolo's lectures. The "unknown" figure she calls Sordello.

[67]

XII

SOCRATES AND ALCIBIADES

In the same room which holds Parnassus, with Poetry above on the ceiling, there is another wall painting by Raphael, which commonly bears the name of The School of Athens, though that name was not originally applied to it. In the ceiling above is a figure representing Philosophy, and the picture below carries out the idea in its presentation of an assembly of scholars.

Just as in Parnassus Raphael brought together as in a beautiful dream the god of poetry, the nine muses, and famous poets of the ancient and what was to him the modern world, so, in the School of Athens, he has assembled a great company of philosophers, chiefly out of the famous line of Greek scholars. In a general way he has divided the assembly into two groups, one of men who devote themselves to pure thought, the other of those who apply their thought to science, like geometry, arithmetic, astronomy, and music.

There are more than fifty figures in this great painting. Raphael has made it clear whom he meant to represent, in many cases. They were the philosophers, whom his friends among the cardinals and learned men were so enthusiastic about. But he has [68] also gathered about these teachers those who might be their pupils; they are in many cases young Italians of his own day; indeed, he has even pictured himself coming in with a fellow artist.

What interested him was to paint a great number of persons who should show by their faces and their attitudes that they were busy, in an animated way, over what was worth thinking about. He placed them in a noble hall, with a domed recess at the end, such as a great architect of his day might have built. He showed a noble colonnade of pillars, and he placed in niches statues of the old Greek gods like Apollo and Minerva, who would be supposed to take an interest in what was going on.

The picture is so large and has so many figures that it would not be easy to reproduce it here, and give a good idea of its various parts; so a portion only is shown, depicting what is commonly known as the group of Socrates and Alcibiades. Socrates can surely be distinguished, for he had a singular face and head. Some have thought the companion was not Alcibiades, but Xenophon.

It does not greatly matter. Each was his companion and pupil, when he was living. Xenophon wrote a narrative of his master's life and death. Alcibiades is often mentioned in the dialogues of Plato, who also has preserved for us the great sayings of Socrates. Two or three men stand about, listening to a discussion which Socrates is having with his companion.

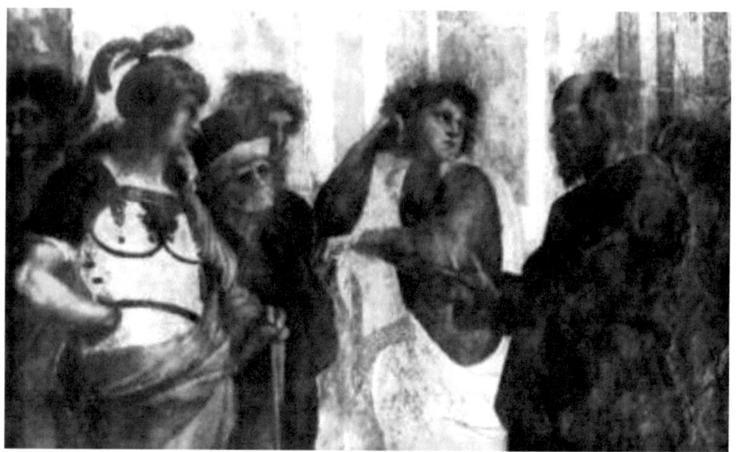

SOCRATES AND ALCIBIADES
Vatican Palace, Rome

Please click on the image for a larger image.

Please click here for a modern color image

The chief interest centres in Socrates, who seems [71] to be explaining his principles, telling them off, one by one, on his fingers. In the old accounts which we have of this philosopher, he is shown to have been a man who had thought deeply about the most important things, but used the plainest, most homely speech when he was trying to make his meaning clear. His plain face and eccentric figure were a familiar sight in the market places, where he used to linger, drawing young men into conversation, by which he tried to show them the better things of life.

Alcibiades was, as Socrates acknowledged, "the fairest and tallest of the citizens;" he was also "among the noblest of them," and the nephew of the powerful Athenian, Pericles. Moreover, he was rich, though this was a smaller matter. All these things, however, had lifted Alcibiades up; and with the vanity of youth, he was ambitious for a great oratorical career, without having in reality any sufficient preparation. It is at this juncture that he falls in with Socrates, who begins to question him kindly about his plans. The young man confesses his ambitions, and the philosopher innocently asks him where and how he has made his preparatory studies. Alcibiades seems to think that the ordinary subjects of oratory, such as questions of war and peace, justice and injustice, need no special knowledge but that learned of the people.

"I cannot say that I have a high opinion of your teachers," says the shrewd old philosopher; "you know that knowledge is the first qualification of any teacher?" [72]

Alcibiades. Certainly.

Socrates. And if they know, they must agree together and not differ?

Alcibiades. Yes.

Socrates. And would you say that they knew the things about which they differ?

Alcibiades. No.

Socrates. Then how can they teach them?

Alcibiades. They cannot. [9]

So little by little, as one question follows another, Alcibiades comes to see that the popular knowledge upon which he depends is a very weak and variable thing. He confesses at last his own folly, and declares his resolution to devote himself to thoughtful study.

[9] From Plato's dialogue, *Alcibiades*, Jowett's translation.

[73]

XIII

THE FLIGHT OF ÆNEAS

In the series of rooms in the Vatican palace, of which one contains Parnassus, and another the Expulsion of Heliodorus and the Liberation of Peter, there is a room, the first of the series, which is called the Room of the Great Fire, because it contains a large picture of the Conflagration in the Borgo.

The Borgo is that quarter of Rome where the Vatican stands, and in the ninth century there was, one day, a great fire there. It was said that the fire was put out by the Pope of that time, Leo IV., who stood in a portico connected with the church of St. Peter, and made the sign of the cross.

Raphael was bidden make a painting upon one wall of the room, which should represent the scene, and in his characteristic fashion he made it to be not merely a copy of what he might suppose the scene to have been; he introduced a poetic element, which at once made the piece a work of great imagination.

A poet, who was describing such an event, might use an illustration from some other great historic fire. He might have said in effect: "In this burning of the Borgo, men could have been seen carrying the aged away on their shoulders, as when in [74] ancient times Troy was burned, and Æneas bore his father Anchises away from the falling timbers."

This is exactly what Raphael did in painting. In the background of the picture is seen Pope Leo IV. with his clergy, in the portico of the old church of St. Peter's. The Pope's hand is raised, making the sign of the cross; on the steps of the church are the people who have fled to it for refuge. On each side of the foreground are burning houses. Men are busy putting out the fire, and women are bringing them water. Other men and women and children are escaping from the flames, and some are heroically saving the weak and helpless.

It is amongst these last that Raphael has placed the group called the Flight of Æneas. The Trojan bears on his shoulders his father, the old, blind Anchises. Behind is Creusa, the wife of Æneas, looking back with terror upon the burning city, and by the side of

Æneas is his young son Iulus, looking up into his face with a trusting gaze.

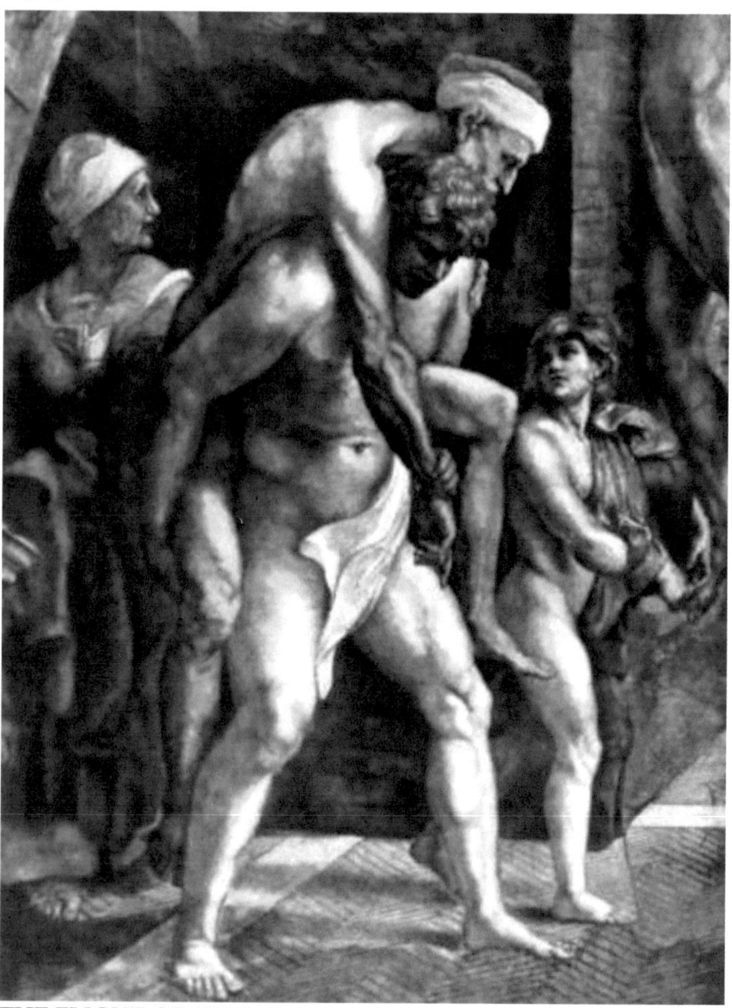

THE FLIGHT OF ÆNEAS
Vatican Palace, Rome

Please click on the image for a larger image.

Some one of Raphael's friends had no doubt told him the story, or read it to him out of Virgil's Æneid, which was one of the favorite books in that day, when men were delighting in the recovery of the great poetry of Greece and Rome. Here is a part of the story as told by Virgil in the translation by C. P. Cranch:—

> "But when I reached my old paternal home,
> My father, whom I wished to bear away
> To the high mountains, and who first of all
> I sought, refused to lengthen out his life,
> And suffer exile, now that Troy was lost.
> [77] 'O ye,' he said, 'whose blood is full of life,
> Whose solid strength in youthful vigor stands,—
> Plan ye your flight! But if the heavenly powers
> Had destined me to live, they would have kept
> For me these seats. Enough, more than enough,
> That one destruction I have seen, and I
> Survive the captured city. Go ye then,
> Bidding this frame farewell—thus, lying thus
> Extended on the earth! I shall find death
> From some hand.'

> 'O father, dost thou think
> That I can go and leave thee here alone?
> Comes such bad counsel from my father's lips?
> If't is the pleasure of the gods that naught
> From the whole city should be left, and this
> Is thy determined thought and wish, to add
> To perishing Troy thyself and all thy kin,—
> The gate lies open for that death desired.'"

So saying, Æneas calls for his arms, resolved to remain with Father Anchises fighting the Greeks to the death. Thereupon Creusa his wife begins to weep, begging him not to leave her and her little boy Iulus to perish in the flames. In the midst of her lamentations a sacred omen is given, in the appearance of lambent flames playing about the head of Iulus. Anchises is convinced of the will of the gods.

"'Now, now,' he cries, 'for us no more delay!
I follow; and wherever ye may lead,
Gods of my country, I will go! Guard ye
My family, my little grandson guard.
This augury is yours; and yours the power
That watches Troy. And now, my son, I yield,
Nor will refuse to go along with thee.'
And now through all the city we can hear
The roaring flames, which nearer roll their heat.
'Come then, dear father! On my shoulders I
[78] Will bear thee, nor will think the task severe.
Whatever lot awaits us, there shall be
One danger and one safety for us both.
Little Iulus my companion be;
And at a distance let my wife observe
Our footsteps.'

This said, a tawny lion's skin
On my broad shoulders and my stooping neck
I throw, and take my burden. At my side
Little Iulus links his hand in mine,
Following his father with unequal steps.
Behind us steps my wife. Through paths obscure
We wend; and I, who but a moment since
Dreaded no flying weapons of the Greeks,
Nor dense battalions of the adverse hosts,
Now start in terror at each rustling breeze,
And every common sound, held in suspense
With equal fears for those attending me,
And for the burden that I bore along."

[79]

XIV

ST. MICHAEL SLAYING THE DRAGON

There are many legends about St. Michael, who is also represent-ed as the Archangel, or head of the whole company of angels, and most of these legends spring from a few passages in the Bible, chiefly two. One of these is in the Epistle of Jude, the ninth verse, where the archangel Michael is alluded to as "contending with the Devil." The other is in the Book of Revelation, beginning at the seventh verse of the ninth chapter: —

"And there was war in heaven: Michael and his angels fought against the dragon; and the dragon fought and his angels, and pre-vailed not; neither was their place found any more in heaven. And the great dragon was cast out, that old serpent called the Devil, and Satan which deceiveth the whole world; he was cast out into the earth, and his angels were cast out with him."

The Book of Revelation is full of strange imagery; and ever since it was written, men learned and unlearned have tried to turn its impassioned verses into real historical scenes, past or to come. Above all, this figure of a dragon, a monster part man, part brute, puzzled people, and they have all sorts of explanations to make of it. [80]

In our fairy tales we often hear of hobgoblins and dragons and like fearful beings, and we think of them as make-believe creatures, and sometimes are afraid of them, even though if we are questioned we say we know they do not really exist. But in Raphael's day, dragons were by no means unreal things to people. Some thought they had seen them, and there were a great many persons who if they had not seen them themselves were sure others had seen them.

In Raphael's day there were large tracts of the world, dark woods, inaccessible mountains, which had hardly been explored at all, and people fancied them haunted by strange men and stranger animals. As more and more light is let into the world, these dark places dis-appear, and we have come to know just what kinds of animals and men there are everywhere. Yet still, we are not quite sure there may not be singular beasts lurking out of sight, like the sea serpent for example.

Now, the dragon in early days stood for what was ugly and terrible and a hater of good. The Greeks believed there were dragons, and they had many tales of how Hercules or this or that hero slew a dragon. To the Christian of the Middle Ages the dragon stood at one end of the scale, an archangel at the other; for as the dragon was all darkness and hideousness, the archangel was all light and beauty and gloriousness. It thrilled every one to think of the angel of light fighting with and overcoming the beast of darkness; for every one knew that sort [81] of struggle was going on in the world, even in himself.

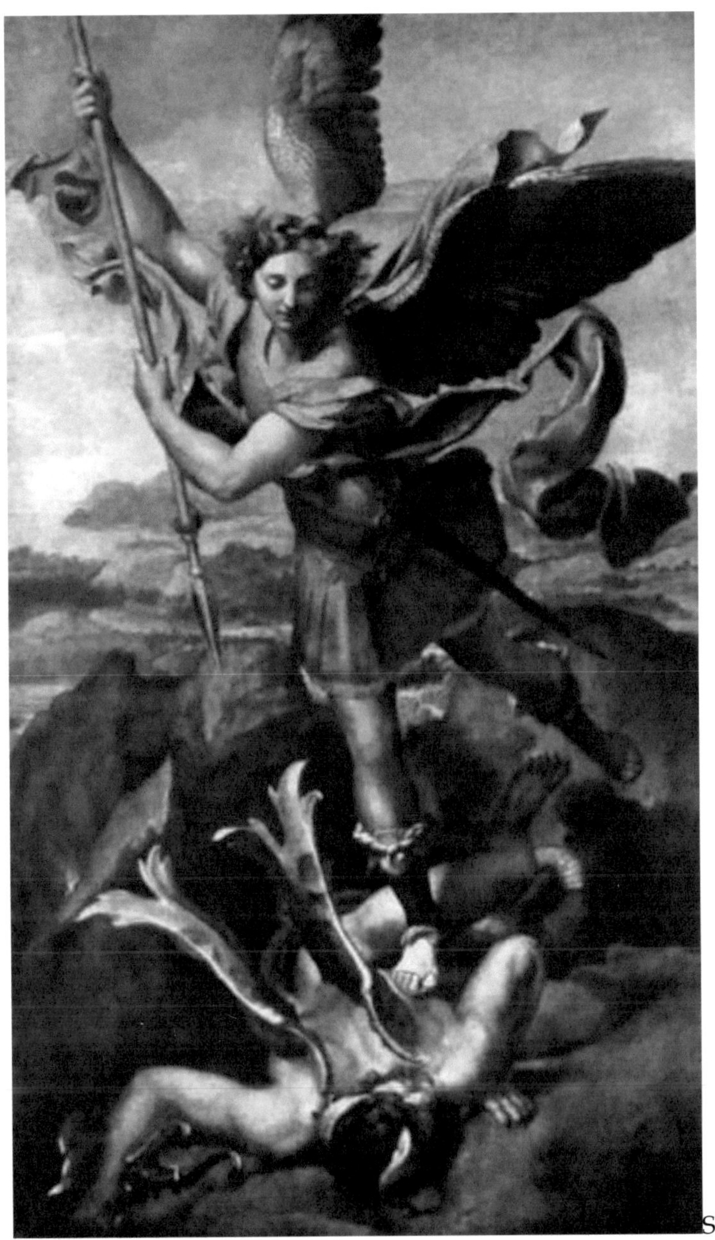

ST.

MICHAEL SLAYING THE DRAGON
The Louvre, Paris

Please click on the image for a larger image.

Please click here for a modern color image

[83]

Raphael's picture gives a fine contrast between the beautiful, strong, young archangel and his ugly foe. St. Michael hovers in mid air as light and graceful as a bird, while Satan squirms beneath his feet, a loathsome creature scorched by the flames and sulphurous fumes, which pour from the clefts of the rock.

In the artist's imagination both are spirits, and so both are winged; for wings, which carry one through the air, naturally are symbols of spiritual existence. But the wings of the archangel are the wings of some great, glorious bird like the eagle, which soars upward toward the sun; the wings of the dragon are more like the wings of a bat, which flies only in darkness and clings to the roofs of caves.

After all, the first and last impression which we get from the picture is the lightning-like movement of the archangel. He darts at the dragon as if he had come from heaven with the swiftness of light, his robe flying like the wind away from him, his wings not spread in flight, but lifted in his poise, and his face bearing the serenity of an assured victory as he lifts his spear for its final thrust.

The great English poet Milton has made use of this same subject in "Paradise Lost." Here is a portion of the story in the sixth book, lines 316-330: —

> "Together both, with next to almighty arm
> Uplifted imminent, one stroke they aimed
> That might determine, and not need repeat
> [84] As not of power, at once; nor odds appeared
> In might or swift prevention.
> But the sword of Michael from the armory of God
> Was given him, tempered so that neither keen
> Nor solid might resist that edge: it met
> The sword of Satan, with steep force to smite

Descending, and in half cut sheer; nor stayed
But with swift wheel reverse, deep entering, shared
All his right side.
Then Satan first knew pain,
And writhed him to and fro convolved; so sore
The griding sword with discontinuous wound
Passed through him."

[85]

XV

THE SISTINE MADONNA

As we turn to the picture, famous the world over as the Sistine Madonna, we seem to be looking through a window opening into heaven. Faint in the background, yet filling the whole space, is a cloud of innumerable cherubs; out of this cloud, and enveloped by it, appear the Mother and Child.

They are taking their way seemingly from heaven to earth. A curtain has been drawn aside that we may see them, and two figures are on either side, as if to await their passing, one gazing into their faces while he points outward, the other also kneeling in devotion yet looking intently down. The mother's robes are blown back by the wind as she moves steadily forward.

Underneath is a parapet, as if this were indeed a window, and two beautiful boy-angels lean upon it, adoration on their faces and rest in their position, as if they were everlastingly praising, and were the very embodiments of cheerful innocence.

It is worth while to look at this picture for a moment, without thinking of its meaning, and indeed without paying much attention to the beauty of the figures, just to see how this great painter has managed the lines and masses of the work. In art, lines [86] and masses and color are not unlike what words and sentences and what we call style are in literature. Even if a writer has good and beautiful ideas, much of the pleasure we might derive is lost when the words are ill chosen, the sentences are bungling, perhaps even ungrammatical, and the whole expression is commonplace or confusing.

We cannot get any notion of Raphael's color from our little print, but it is not difficult to trace the lines and to see something of the effect of the masses, and of light and shade. The shape of the whole is a combination of pyramids. When you see the great base of a pyramid and observe how the sides taper upward, you are aware that nothing could stand more securely and at the same time suggest lightness, by the rising and receding of the sides.

Now here you see that lines drawn from the shoulders of the two attendant figures would meet at the Virgin's head, as at the apex of a pyramid. The curtains even help this effect, by being drawn aside in such a way as to make these lines more evident.

In the lower half of the picture the lines in the draperies of the kneeling saints taper to an imaginary point between the heads of the cherubs, forming a second inverted pyramid or triangle. Thus the composition is inclosed in a harmonious figure whose outlines suggest what we call a diamond.

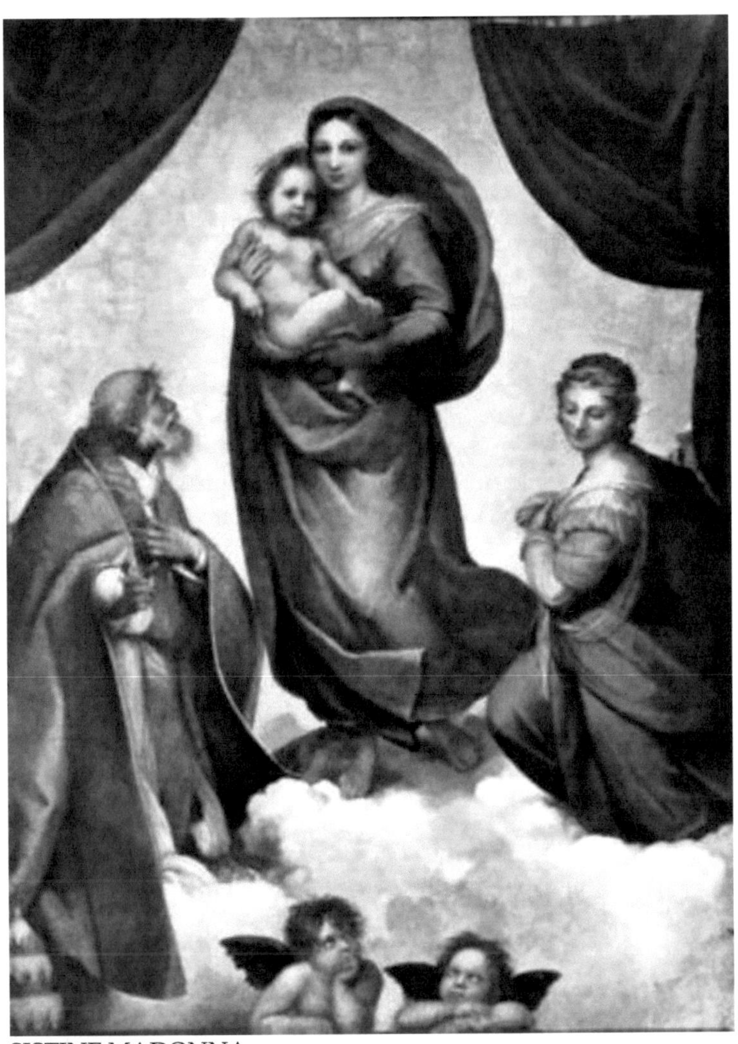

SISTINE MADONNA
Dresden Gallery

Please click on the image for a larger image.

Please click here for a modern color image

Perhaps one reason why a triangular arrangement satisfies the eye, lies in the simple fact that the most important and yet familiar object in nature is thus [89] arranged. Thus in this picture, the three principal persons form the upper triangle, and the body of each person repeats the figure, — that is, the head rises from the shoulders in such a way that the lines inclosing them produce a triangle. Further, in each face, the line formed by the eyes is connected by two imaginary lines meeting at the mouth.

In the picture the central figure illustrates this very noticeably. The arm of the Virgin forms by its position, along with the body of the child, a base, from which two other lines rise, tapering to the top of the head; the child's head lies right in the course of one of these lines. Thus mother and child together form a single figure, the two united in one.

But when we have studied this simple principle of composition, we go back with delight to the picture itself for what it tells us: the deep mystery of the mother's face, as if she were lifted above the ordinary plane of human life; the blended loveliness of childhood with the consciousness of a holy calling; the lowly devotion yet dignity of St. Barbara; the grandeur and forgetfulness of self of the Pope, whose triple crown rests on the parapet; the perpetual childhood of the angelic figures.

The picture takes its name from the Pope, who had been canonized as St. Sixtus. It was painted for the convent of St. Sixtus at Piacenza, but early in the eighteenth century it was bought by the Elector of Saxony, and now hangs in the gallery at Dresden. It is a pleasant thing to know that when Frederick the Great bombarded Dresden, he ordered [90] his cannon to keep clear of the Picture Gallery. Napoleon, too, though he took many pictures to Paris, did not take any from the Dresden gallery.

When we compare the Sistine Madonna with the Madonna of the Chair, we see what a wide variety of pictures there may be on the single subject of the Mother and Child. The Madonna of the Chair is, as we have said, a home scene, like a picture from real life. The

Sistine Madonna is a vision; the figures are lifted above the actual surroundings of earth into a purely ideal and heavenly atmosphere. In the Madonna of the Chair, the Mother and Child are all in all to each other, and what attracts us most in the picture is the mother's love. In the other picture both mother and boy seem to forget themselves in the thought of some glorious service to others.

[91]

XVI

PORTRAIT OF RAPHAEL

We have been looking at fifteen pictures designed by Raphael. They are but a few of the great number painted either wholly or in part by the master, or painted by his pupils from designs and sketches made by him. He was thirty-seven years old when he died, and it was said that he died on his birthday. His life was brimful of activity as a painter.

The portrait which stands at the beginning of this little book was painted by himself at the age of twenty-three, for his mother's brother, whom he was wont to call his "second father." An English poet, Samuel Rogers, in his poem "Italy," has these lines which describe it prettily: —

> "His heavenly face a mirror of his mind,
> His mind a temple for all lovely things
> To flock to and inhabit."

One of his contemporaries, Vasari, wrote a book of "Lives of the Painters," and thus he speaks of Raphael: "All confessed the influence of his sweet and gracious nature, which was so replete with excellence, and so perfect in all the charities, that not only was he honored by men, but even by the very animals, who would constantly follow his steps, and always loved him." [92]

If we think of what was happening to Raphael in the year 1506, when he painted this portrait, perhaps we shall read more truthfully the expression in his face. Seven years before he had entered the studio of Perugino, and had begun to learn from that master and to show something of his own power. Two years before he had made his first visit to Florence, and there he saw some of the great pictures by Leonardo da Vinci and Michael Angelo, and had a new conception of what art could do.

He had already shown the effect upon him in some of his greatest Madonnas, and he stood now on the threshold of a great career.

New ambitions awoke within him; new ideals flashed upon his inner vision. Modest and gentle though he was, he felt a growing consciousness of his own power.

So he holds his head high; not haughtily, but with a dignified self-confidence. His eyes seem to see the visions of which he dreams; his mouth is half parted as if in expectancy. Happy and lovable, there is a sweet thoughtfulness in his air which gives promise of his wonderful performance.

[93]

PRONOUNCING VOCABULARY OF PROPER NAMES AND FOREIGN WORDS

The Diacritical Marks given are those found in the latest edition of Webster's International Dictionary.

EXPLANATION OF DIACRITICAL MARKS.

A Dash (¯) above the vowel denotes the long sound, as in fāte, ēve, tīme, nōte, ūse.

A Curve (˘) above the vowel denotes the short sound, as in ădd, ĕnd, ĭll, ŏdd, ŭp.

A Dot (˙) above the vowel a denotes the obscure sound of a in paˑst, aˑbāte, Amĕricaˑ.

A Double Dot (¨) above the vowel a denotes the broad sound of a in fäther, älms.

A Double Dot (..) below the vowel a denotes the sound of a in ba̤ll.

A Wave (~) above the vowel e denotes the sound of e in hẽr.

A Circumflex Accent (^) above the vowel o denotes the sound of o in bôrn.

é sounds like e in dḗpĕnd.

ó sounds like o in prŏpōse.

ç sounds like s.

c sounds like k.

ṣ sounds like z.

ḡ is hard as in ḡet.

ġ is soft as in ġem.

- Aeneas (ḗ n $\overline{oo}$ às).
- Alcibiades (Ălçĭbĭȧdēz).
- Anchises (ăn kī́ s $\overline{oo}$ z).

- Apocrypha (à pŏḱrĭ fà).
- Apollo (A̓pŏ́llō).
- Arras (Ärräś).
- Augustine (á̇g̅ŭs t ōōn).

- Barnabas (Bär̓nàbàs).
- Borgo (Bôr̓g̅ō).

- Calliope (cǎllĭ́ŏ́pě́).
- Costis (cŏśtĭs).
- Creusa (crēū́sà).

- Dante (Dǎńtě́).

- Elias (É̇lĭ́às).
- Elijah (É̇lĭ́jah).

- Galilee (Gǎ́lĭl ōō).
- Gennesaret (Gĕnnĕśàrĕt).
- Gentiles (Gĕńtīlȩs).

- Heliodorus (Hēlĭ̆ōdŏ́rŭs).
- Hercules (Hĕŕcūlȩ̄s).
- Herod (Hĕŕŏd).
- Hippocrene (Hĭ̇ppōcrĕ́ně́).

- Iulus (Iū́lŭs).

- Josephus (jō s ōōfŭs).

- Leonardo da Vinci (lā ō när̓dō dä vĭ́ńch ōō).
- Loggia (lŏd̓jà).
- Louvre (l o̅o̅́vr).

- Lycaonia (līk ȧ ṓnĭ ȧ).
- Lystra (Ly̆strȧ).

- Maccabees (măḱ ȧ b ōō z).
- Madame (Mădämé).
- Magdalene (Măǵ dā̇lĕn).
- Mamre (Măḿ rē).
- Maximin (Măx̌ĭmĭn).
- Melchisedec (mĕl kǐź ḗ dĕk). [94]
- Mercurius (Mĕrcúrĭŭs).
- Minerva (Mĭnẽŕvȧ).

- Onias (O̱níȧs).

- Parnassus (Pärnăśsŭs).
- Pericles (Pĕrǐclẹs).
- Perugino (pā r ōō j ōō nō).
- Piacenza (Pē ä chĕń dzä).
- Pindar (Pǐńdär).
- Plato (Plắtō).
- Plautus (Plạ́ṭŭs).
- Polymnia (Pṓly̆ḿnĭȧ).

- Raphael (Rắfāĕl).

- Sabinella (Săbǐnĕ́llȧ).
- Sappho (sắffō).
- Sheba (Shébȧ).
- Signora (S ōō n yṓrȧ).
- Sinai (Sīńī).
- Sistine (Sǐśt ōō n).
- Socrates (Sŏćrȧtē̱s).
- Sodom (Sŏd́ŏm).
- Stanza dEliodoro (Ständzä dā lḗ ṓ dṓ rō).

- Urban (Ur̄ban).
- Urbino ($\overline{OO}$ r b $\overline{oo}$ nō).

- Vasari (vä sä r $\overline{oo}$).
- Vatican (Văt́ĭcăn).

- Xenophon (zĕńố fŏn).

- Zebedee (Zĕbĕd $\overline{oo}$).